Charles Edwin Taylor

An Island of the Sea

Descriptive of the Past and Present of St. Thomas, Danish West Indies

Charles Edwin Taylor

An Island of the Sea
Descriptive of the Past and Present of St. Thomas, Danish West Indies

ISBN/EAN: 9783744733472

Printed in Europe, USA, Canada, Australia, Japan

Cover: Foto ©Andreas Hilbeck / pixelio.de

More available books at **www.hansebooks.com**

DESCRIPTIVE OF THE

PAST AND PRESENT OF ST. THOMAS, DANISH WEST INDIES.

WITH

A FEW SHORT STORIES ABOUT BLUEBEARD'S AND BLACKBEARD'S CASTLES.

BY

CHAS. EDWIN TAYLOR, M.D., F.R.G.S.,

Member of the Colonial Council of St. Thomas and St. John, of the Board of Health and Hospital Commission; Fellow and Honorary Member of various Scientific and Literary Societies in Europe, Asia, and America. Author of " Leaflets from the Danish

ALL RIGHTS RESERVED.

LONDON:
EYRE AND SPOTTISWOODE,
Her Majesty's Printers,
DOWNS PARK ROAD, HACKNEY, N.E.

PREFACE.

Of late years tourists are beginning to find their way to the West Indies. Their mild and equable climate, beautiful scenery, the hospitable character of their inhabitants, are thus becoming known; and as time rolls on, these islands will become as frequented as other routes of travel, recommended as interesting and delightful to invalids and pleasure seekers. Most of the steamship lines bringing them call at St. Thomas. It is generally the first glimpse they get of West Indian life, its picturesque town and romantic old towers always exciting their curiosity. For such as these this book has been written, for in it will be found almost everything that is known about them. Should anything be omitted, it is to be hoped that some excuse will be found; one cannot always particularize, especially where the exact items are wanting. The illustrations will, no doubt, recommend themselves. They are reproduced from photographs by our local artists, to whom the thanks of the writer are due for their kind permission to use them.

To those who have encouraged him to bring out "An Island of the Sea," he begs to express his gratitude and sincere appreciation.

And now, having got through the most difficult part of his book, he begs to subscribe himself most faithfully,

THE AUTHOR.

August 31*st*, 1895.

PREFACE TO THE SECOND EDITION.

THE favourable reception which the first edition of this work has met with at the hands of an appreciative public has induced me to issue a second, with the addition of a few words about St. Croix, "The Garden of the West Indies." This, I trust, will be acceptable to those who desire to know more about these beautiful "Isles of the Sea." There is so much to be said of their attractions, bright spots, and romantic history, that whole volumes might be written about them. If I have not been able to say more of them in this, it must be attributed to the expense which such a work would entail, rather than to any design of mine to leave anything unsaid to their advantage. Some day, perhaps, I may bring out a third and improved edition. This, however, depends upon the approval of my readers. Till then, with thanks for past favours, I have the honour to subscribe myself,

THE AUTHOR.

St. Thomas, *June* 1896.

CONTENTS.

PART I.
	PAGE
THE PAST	7

PART II.
THE PRESENT	28

PART III.
STORIES OF BLUEBEARD'S AND BLACKBEARD'S CASTLES.

"Bluebeard's Casket"	45
"A Remarkable Coincidence"	59
"Black Ivory"	74
"James Teach's Doubloons"	91
"An Old Colonial Governor"	102

CHARLES EDWIN TAYLOR, M.D.

AN ISLAND OF THE SEA.

PART I.

THE PAST.

I AM going to tell you about "An Island of the Sea," one of those islands that Columbus discovered on his second voyage to the West Indies, in the year 1493. There are many others more populous, more extensive, more richly endowed by Nature, perhaps, but few of them can boast of such a career of prosperity, the latter part of which is yet within the memory of some of us.

And what memories does a voyage on the waters of the Blue Caribbean recall to you. Not an island that you touch at, but reminds you of some deed of valour done by brave seamen, some wild story of the days when "El Draque,"* as the Spaniards called him, was the terror of this azure-tinted sea.

You read of Jamaica, now prosperous and successful as a great fruit-growing country, sending its luscious products weekly to America; of Trinidad's activity, its wondrous pitch lake, botanical gardens, its yearly exports of millions of pounds of "cocoa"; of Grenada's fertile valleys, its productions of cotton, spices, and coffee; of St. Vincent, with its *Souffrière*, and as the "island of arrowroot"; of St. Lucia's future prospects; of Dominica's luxuriant vegetation, virgin forests, deep ravines and lofty wooded mountains, its timber and countless natural products; of Montserrat, with its lime trees and export trade of lime juice; of Antigua, the puzzle of geologists and the home of important public institutions; of St. Kitt's and Nevis, with their sugar cultivation, and of the Virgin Islands. And if you are not tired you may read of that ancient colony, Barbados, with its enormous population, busy as bees from morn till night, among its lovely plantations or in its bustling city; of

---
* Sir Francis Drake.

St. Domingo and Hayti, still struggling in the throes of a despotism perhaps necessary to their progress, or of Cuba, where its natives emulous of their neighbours' independence are arrayed in arms against the Spaniards, battling for their liberty.

Yes! you may read of all these lovely fertile, smiling islands, where God's precious sunlight kisses their mountain tops nearly every morning of their existence, but in few volumes will you find anything about the "Island of the Sea," of which I have promised to tell you, and which, if smaller than most of them, has none the less left its mark upon the pages of West Indian history. And it is to a little Danish colony I am going to devote a few chapters of this book, colonized by Danes from the beginning, the white-crossed, blood-red banner of the Dannebrog yet floats over it, and seems likely to, if America or Germany, which, more than once have cast longing eyes towards it, do not some day exchange it for their own.

And now you may have guessed that my "Island of the Sea," is St. Thomas, once named "The Emporium of the Antilles."

In a former work * I have endeavoured to sketch its history. Here it is only possible, briefly to recapitulate and in bringing it up to date, to notice its past and present position, and some of the causes which may have led to its decadence as a commercial centre.

That this island must have existed far back in the mists of ages, its formation plainly shows. Of the cataclysm, which caused it to spring into existence, we have no information. Amidst volcanic fires, geology tells us, it must have been evolved, and it is quite possible that, some day, it may disappear beneath the ocean under the same conditions.

We are pretty sure that the Caribs inhabited it at one time. Numerous stone chisels have been found in different parts of the island, and there are yet some curious carvings on some rocks in the neighbouring island of St. John, which strongly confirm the assertion.

What we do know is, that Erik Smidt, the Dane, arrived at St. Thomas on the morning of the 30th of March 1666, in a ship called "De Eendracht," took possession of it for Denmark, landed a small colony, which suffered great privations, and died shortly after his arrival.

---

* "Leaflets from the Danish West Indies."

Then a Dutch Governor, named Huntum, when the settlement was in sore straits for provisions, landed in force and broke it up.

So that the actual history of St. Thomas cannot be said to have commenced before the time that Jórgen Iwersen became its Governor on the 23rd of May 1672, when he came there as chief of an expedition sent out from Copenhagen by the Danish West India and Guinea Company. An idea of his iron-handed rule may be formed from the story of "An Old Colonial Governor," which is to be found within these pages. With "Christian's Fort," completed some time after his arrival, and some 50 estates under cultivation, it may be said that its population of 331 souls, black and white, was fairly prospering, and it was unfortunate, perhaps, that Jórgen Iwersen's rule came shortly to an end, he being superseded at his own request by one "Nic Esmit," only to be thrown overboard by a mutinous crew on his re-appointment as Governor and return to the island of St. Thomas.

Slavery appears already to have existed in the colony, both white and black; but, encouraged by King Christian V., a great number of negroes were brought from Africa, and the cultivation of sugar was introduced.

Four Governors had already ruled St. Thomas, when a violent earthquake took place on a Sunday, the 9th of April, in the year 1690. It cracked the walls of many buildings, and the sea receded so that the fish could be picked up from the bottom, nine or ten fathoms out.

It is about this time that we first hear of Bluebeard's Castle, which was then known as Frederik's Fort, built upon Smith's Hill in 1689, by Government.

It seems sad to sweep away the halo of romance with which imagination has invested it, but the fact is there, though the pen of fiction has told a score of stories about it and its sister tower, named after Blackbeard.

Very shortly afterwards the King of Denmark farmed out the island to one George Thormohlen, a little before the Brandenburgh Company had established itself with certain rights and privileges.

On the 31st of March 1692 the first regular troops were garrisoned in the island. In those days the colonists objected to taxation, and when asked for the support of the soldiers, they steadily refused. Nor do we find that it was ever enforced.

In 1694 Thormohlen was replaced by De La Vigne, who, in his turn, was superseded by Governor Lorentz, under whose rule we find the first severe hurricane recorded. This was in 1697.

In 1701 Pere Labat visited the island. In his interesting book on the West Indies * he gives a fair picture of St. Thomas. Of its commerce he makes these remarks:—

"Denmark being almost neutral in the wars of Europe, the port of St. Thomas is open to all nations. During peace it serves as an *entrepôt* for the commerce which the French, English, Spaniards and Dutch do not dare to pursue openly on their own islands; and in time of war, it is the refuge of merchant ships when pursued by privateers. On the other hand, the privateers send their prizes here to be sold when they are not disposed to send them to a greater distance. Many small vessels proceed from St. Thomas to the coast of South America, whence they bring back much riches in the form of specie or in bars and valuable merchandize. In a word, St. Thomas is a market of consequence."

Thus we see, even at this early period, that prosperity was dawning for this "Island of the Sea." Its geographical position, and its magnificent harbour, though as yet destitute of wharves and those great facilities which, in later years, have made it almost unique in the West Indies, were already giving it a commercial importance which belonged to no other island.

It is pleasant to look through the pages of the good father, and read his lifelike description of the little town now known as Charlotte Amalia.

Consisting of one street only, it followed the contour of the bay, which terminated in the factory or offices of the Company. This was a large and handsome edifice, with many apartments and magazines for the storage of merchandize. Here they secured the slaves, in which a large trade was done with the Spaniards. The houses, which were formerly nothing but huts, were built of bricks. He speaks of two small streets to the right of the factory, which were filled with French refugees. He does not tell us where they came from, nor have I been able to find out. Most all the houses were of one storey and

---

* "Voyage aux Iles de l'Amérique," Vol. II., page 285.

very well arranged, their pavement being of tiles and the interiors whitewashed.

He also speaks favorably of its agriculture. The estates though small were well kept. The soil, if light, was good, producing an abundance of manioc, millet, sweet potatoes, and all kinds of fruits and herbs. The sugar cane grew well. They had few cows and horses, for lack of pasturage; but the inhabitants did not want for meat, the Spaniards furnishing them with it in abundance. Young kids and fowls were raised in quantities. Provisions were always dear, but money was plentiful, strangers arriving in affluence.

A brilliant picture for so short an existence the colony had passed through; and as our "Island of the Sea" went on progressing through the years that followed, under several Governors, during which the cultivation of indigo was commenced, another frightful hurricane devastated it. This was in 1713.

In 1716, the import duties were changed from six to eight per cent., congregations were permitted to elect their own pastors, and the Secret Council was now separated from the courts in which they formerly sat as judges. About this time a deputation was sent home to Copenhagen, the first Government House was purchased, and the privileges of the Brandenburgh Company ceased. Then a land tax was imposed and a tax of two and a half rix dollars for each man, woman, and slave.

Then a Royal Council administered the affairs of the colony. It consisted of five persons besides the Governor, as President, two merchants, the bookkeeper, treasurer, and secretary. Planters had no more the power of life and death over their slaves, and were bound to treat them well. Clerks serving six years were then permitted to return home; but young unmarried women were not to enjoy the privilege at all, without special permission, a state of things our young ladies of to-day will surely smile at.

A Reconciling Court, with the Governor as judge, was now established, and the duties on imports and exports were lowered to five or six per cent. St. Thomas was in a flourishing condition. Untold wealth flowed to its shores, and it was not until the year 1756 that its very existence was threatened by the very means that had contributed to its greatness.

Up to this time the Dutch had carried on a great trade in St. Thomas. The Company, jealous of their success, united with the merchants, and with their help proceeded to exclude the Dutch from all commerce with the colonies.

It had now become a gigantic monopoly, which from the oppressive restrictions it put upon the island for its own special benefit, soon promised its extinction.

It was then that His Majesty, King Frederik V., stepped in and acquired all its privileges by purchase. It was an enormous price they obtained for them, but no price was too great to pay to get rid of what, at the time, was a curse instead of a benefit. Unfortunately for the colony, such a sweeping change brought misery, and it is recorded that emigration was of daily occurrence, money became scarce, a paper currency was issued, and of the few inhabitants left to sustain its fallen fortunes the majority were slaves.

Only on the 9th of April 1764, when it was declared a free port for vessels of all nations, did its star become once more in the ascendant. Ships came in, and with them the money so much needed.

The history of St. Thomas, from that date, is a long record of triumphant progress in commerce and industry. Its harbour was full of ships, its town grew rapidly, great houses were established, wealthy merchants came there to remain, and from morn till eve its stores were alive with busy purchasers.

The first rude shock came with the English, who blockaded it in the year 1800. Denmark was at war with Great Britain. So, on the 1st of April 1801, our "Island of the Sea" surrendered to a military and naval force under Colonel Cowell. For ten months they held it, when it was restored to Denmark, on the 22nd of Feb. 1802. During this time its commerce was at a standstill.

Destructive fires took place in 1804 and 1806, which destroyed over 16,000,000 dollars worth of property, and in 1807, the island was again surrendered to the English, who occupied it till the 9th of April 1815, when they restored it to Denmark, and its trade again revived.

On the 4th of July 1848 the freedom of the slaves was proclaimed at the drum-head. From that day agriculture became a dead letter in St. Thomas, and of the 90 estates, which 100 years ago were under cultivation, none remain except in name. From this time, however, our "Island of the Sea" prospered greatly, gold flowed into the coffers of its merchants, and plenty reigned in every household.

On Nov. 15th, 1863, King Frederik VII., so beloved by all his subjects, passed to a higher life. His Majesty, the present King, succeeded him. Shortly after his accession to the throne, the Colonial Law came into force, April 1864, the harbour was dredged out, a fine marine repairing slip was in operation, 1600 shares in an iron Floating Dock were subscribed for, Gas Works were planned, and a new Government House, a Custom House, Public Wharf, new Lighthouse, and a Fish Market were to be erected.

The war between the Northern and Southern States of America brought blockade runners to the port, and, as a consequence, more wealth. Another war, in which the hearts of the people were deeply concerned, was being fought at home between Denmark and Germany.

The "Clara Rothe," a steamer of 366 tons, now ran between St. Thomas and St. Croix.* On the 8th of April 1865, the corner-stone of the new Government House was laid. On the 9th of Jan. 1866, the Hon. W. H. Seward, Secretary of State for the United States of America, visited the island. Rumours were then circulated that America was desirous of acquiring St. Thomas as a coaling station.

At this time, the town was in a very unhealthy condition. Small-pox and yellow fever had existed for some months, and on the 18th of Nov. the cholera broke out. It caused 860 deaths.

On the 20th of July 1867 the Floating Dock was inaugurated by being lowered, and the steamship "Wye" was taken in, but the Dock would not come up, and it was not successfully raised and completed till some years afterwards.

To complete the troubles which were now falling thickly round our "Island of the Sea," a terrific hurricane passed over it on the 29th of Oct. More than 300 lives were lost, and 77 vessels were stranded or wrecked. Following this, came the earthquake and tidal wave on the 18th of Nov. These awful calamities were but the beginning of

---

* This service is now done by the "Vigilant," a fast sailing schooner, whose history dates back a hundred years. The "Clara Rothe" ceased plying between the islands, as it did not pay.

the end which awaited St. Thomas, and following each other so rapidly, spread dismay into the stoutest heart. Shortly after these events, and when the outlook seemed most gloomy, the hopes of the people were raised by the prospect of annexation to the United States of America.

The situation is best expressed in the words of Mr. F. A. Ober, an American author, whose books on the West Indies and the Spanish Main * are the delight of everyone who reads them:—

"Unfortunately, our Government once treated with Denmark for this very possession (St. Thomas), the treaty was not only ready for ratification, but the King of Denmark had taken farewell of his loyal subjects and virtually given up the island, when occurred one of those humiliating episodes that more than once have made America a byword in diplomatic circles."

"The treaty intention was ignored: the King of Denmark had the humiliation of recalling his loyal but disappointed subjects, and the attitude of the Home Government towards us cannot be but that of deep resentment. As it stands now, Denmark, though anxious to dispose of her West India possessions, cannot take the initiative, having once been insulted, and has every reason to view with distrust any proposition emanating from the Government of the United States, even should our legislators have the wisdom to move for their acquisition."

More can scarcely be said on a subject reflecting so little credit upon American diplomacy. That the people who had voted for and expected so much from the change, were downcast and dispirited at such a disappointment, cannot be doubted. But the necessity of taking up their burden, and facing the troubles which now awaited them, was manifest, and so we see them once more breasting the waves of adversity which were now setting so strongly against them.

On the 11th of Feb. 1871 the seat of Government was removed from St. Croix to St. Thomas. On the 26th of that month, His Excellency Governor W. L. Birch, Commander of Dannebrog and Dannebrogsmand, died suddenly. On the 30th, His Excellency Chamberlain Franz Ernest Bille, K.D., arrived

* "Camps in the Caribbees." "In the Wake of Columbus."

SOLDIER BAY.

LIGHTHOUSE

in St. Thomas, as Commissioner Extraordinary and Governor of the Danish West Indies. He was to reside at St. Thomas. On the 3rd of August a change in the Police system was inaugurated by the acting Policemaster, Mr. Fischer. On the 23rd of Oct. a frightful hurricane took place. Many lives were lost, and many persons were wounded. Much property was destroyed. On the 16th of Feb. 1872 telegraphic communication was established throughout the line to Havana, and thence to the United States, and thence to Europe.

A new Lighthouse was erected on Muhlensfeldt Point on the 10th of June, and on the 1st of July a dinner was given to His Excellency Governor Bille, by the Colonial Council, on the eve of his departure. His Excellency Governor Stakemann succeeded him *ad interim*.

His Excellency Governor Garde arrived on the 24th of Sept. 1872. Many events of minor importance took place in the years which followed. H.B.M.S. "Challenger" paid a visit to the island, the official paper *St. Thomæ Tidende* changed hands, a rival paper, the *St. Thomas Times*, appeared, the "Apollo Theatre" was opened, and for the first time in its existence the Colonial Council was dissolved. This took place on Jan. 9th, 1875. Many improvements were made under the administration of Governor Garde. On the morning of the 2nd of Dec. 1875 the Floating Dock was tested, and was pronounced a success. A Central Factory was projected for St. Croix, and His Excellency left on the 5th of Jan. 1876 for Denmark, in order to carry it to a successful completion.

Only a few days before his return another frightful hurricane took place, this time including St. Croix, where the damage was very great. Nothing daunted, in face of so many misfortunes, the people took heart of grace, improved their town, established compulsory education, free schools, a fine College, an efficient Quarantine, a thorough system of sanitation, and entering the Postal Union, placed St. Thomas as much ahead of its neighbours as the cleanest and best regulated town in the West Indies, as it had formerly been the most commercial. Then came the visit of H.R.H. Prince Valdemar, the youngest child of King Christian IX., who arrived here as lieutenant on board H.M. corvette "Dagmar," Commander Braem, on the 27th of Sept.

He was the first Danish Prince who had trod West Indian soil, and as such, was received with such demonstrations of loyalty and affection as had never been tendered to anyone before.

In the year 1880 a census was taken of the Danish West Indies, showing the population of St. Thomas to be 14,387. On the 18th of March 1881 His Excellency Governor Garde announced to the Colonial Council of St. Thomas and St. John his resignation of the Governorship, and the appointment of his successor, Colonel C. H. Arendrup, K.D., R.E.

His Excellency Governor Garde left St. Thomas with his family on the 9th of April 1881. Our "Island of the Sea" has had few Governors like him. Alive always to its best interests, earnestly desirous of its prosperity, his memory too is ever green in the hearts of its inhabitants.

Now came His Excellency Colonel C. H. Arendrup, K.D., R.E., on the 15th of April. One of his first acts, shortly after his arrival, was to lay the corner-stone of the Moravian Memorial Church. On Dec. 6th the Transit of Venus was successfully observed by the Brazilian Expedition sent to the island for the purpose. The 31st of March 1883 saw the closing of the College. As nothing to equal it has been put in its place, parents who cannot afford to send their children to Europe for a higher education are obliged to be content with that which the private schools can afford to give them.

In this year an attempt was made to revive the sugar industry, but ended in failure, after several thousands of dollars had been expended. Barbados now threatened to become a formidable rival to St. Thomas. With an empty port, and stores fast closing up, the prospects did not look cheering for our "Island of the Sea." Mexican silver, worth at most 75 to 80 cents, was passing current at the fictitious value of one hundred.

A change was now made in the administration. His Excellency the Governor was to reside six months in St. Thomas and six months in St. Croix. On the 21st of Feb. 1885 a petition was addressed to His Majesty, representing the fallen fortunes of the island, asking the mother country to assume the military expenses and the pensions. On the 1st of July the Royal Mail Steam Packet Company removed its headquarters to Barbados. On the 1st of Dec. the new Harbour and Customs Law came into

CONVENT DES SACRÉS CŒURS.

MORAVIAN MEMORIAL CHURCH.

force. It offered exceptional advantages to vessels seeking the port. For this concession the merchants, through their representatives in Council, allowed the duties to be raised to two per cent. *ad* two per cent. *ad valorem*.

On the 31st of March 1886 a public dinner was given to His Honour Policemaster Fischer on the occasion of his jubilee. No such compliment had been paid before to any official. Dec. 20th of the same year brought a visit from the son of the Crown Prince, who arrived here on board H.M.S. "Jylland." This gave occasion for another display of the people's affection and loyalty towards the Royal House of Denmark. His departure, which took place on the 21st of Feb. 1887, found business pretty brisk. This, however, did not last very long. The hurricane months, with their accustomed dulness, set in, and the end of the year saw our "Island of the Sea" with a depreciated currency and its harbour almost empty.

This brings us to the year 1888, when trade suddenly revived. The harbour was crowded with shipping, and something like activity in business circles prevailed. St. Thomas could now for the first time boast of a Humane Society, founded by a few men who saw the necessity of such an Institution for the prevention of cruelty to animals. This was followed by the inauguration of a Home for Destitute Children. On the 14th of April, His Excellency Governor Arendrup and Mrs. Arendrup celebrated their Silver Wedding; the occasion was commemorated by a superb gift of pure silver from their numerous friends, with a suitable inscription. On the 15th of Nov., the 25th anniversary of the accession to the throne of Their Majesties the King and Queen of Denmark, was celebrated in St. Thomas. Two days were set apart to do honour to the occasion, and it must be said that never in the island's history had anything been seen like the preparations which were made for it. There was booming of cannon in the early morn; services were held in churches. There were chiming of bells and a procession such as the island had never seen before. Everyone had been asked to participate, and every body, corporate and otherwise, were asked to attend. His Excellency the Vice-Governor and Mrs. Andersen assisted, His Excellency Governor Arendrup and Mrs. Arendrup then being abroad in Europe. Orations were made, odes were sung, children were feasted, the poor were dined, boat-races were run. A levée was held, free dances were given, the town was illuminated, and there was such a torchlight procession to conclude with, as will live in the memory of everyone who took part in it, and not a solitary case of disorder was reported; not even a brawl, such was the desire to celebrate, in a becoming manner, the Jubilee of Their Majesties.

On the 27th of Nov. another Jubilee was kept, this time by the Colonial Council, in commemoration of the 25th anniversary of the promulgation of the Colonial Law given by His Majesty King Christian IX.

Shortly after these events, came the news that His Excellency had been decorated in Copenhagen with the Order of Commander of Dannebrog of the first class, and that His Excellency Acting Vice-Governor Andersen had been decorated with the silver cross of Dannebrog. This year closed with the royal thanks to the Jubilee Committee and the royal appreciation of the people's loyalty.

On the 26th of Jan. 1889 His Excellency Governor C. H. Arendrup returned from Europe. About this time the difficulties arising out of the circulation of Mexican silver, and its constant depreciation in value, called for the serious attention of the merchants, and several petitions were got up and presented to the Colonial Council on the subject. On the 4th of Sept. the island was visited by a hurricane, which, though not so disastrous as those of former years, caused a great deal of apprehension and serious damage. As customary, this was taken advantage of by some of its neighbours to injure the place, forgetting that St. Thomas, as a rule, is comparatively free from such visitors, as a glance at the record of any other island in the West Indies will show.

On the 18th of Oct. an alteration in the Colonial Law for the Danish West India Islands, dated 27th of Nov. 1863, was introduced by Government. From what was stated at the time, it appeared that as the island could no longer defray its expenses, and the Budgets showed large deficits, and St. Thomas had become a heavy debtor to the State, the Draft was brought forward with the object of ameliorating the condition of affairs. As a majority of the Members did not view it in the same light as the Government it was strongly opposed in the discussions which followed, and finally rejected.

On the 2nd of July 1890 His Honour Judge P. M. Andersen, K.D. and D.M., ex-Chief Justice of the Royal West India Court, accompanied by his wife, arrived from St. Croix, on his way home for good. His Honour had on more than one occasion filled the post of Vice-Governor during the Governor's absence, and by his tact and courtesy, had earned the good will and esteem of a large circle of friends and the public. On the 13th of Oct., 20 privates and non-commissioned officers, under Acting Captain Paludan, proceeded to Road Town, Tortola, its President having requested the assistance of our local Government to keep the peace among its inhabitants, who had made a hostile demonstration, owing to the prohibitory dues levied on that island. A British sloop-of-war arriving a few days after relieved the Danish soldiers, who returned to St. Thomas in H.B.M.S. "Tourmaline."

On the 19th of Nov. a Draft of Ordinance was introduced into the Colonial Council by one of its members for the alteration of Ordinance, 23rd of Oct. 1885, concerning Custom House duties and Ships' dues. It asked that the Lighthouse dues be abolished altogether, rendering the harbour virtually free to all vessels, seeking, neither discharging cargo nor loading, or only to buy coal or provisions. This move in the right direction, which was loudly called for, in face of the inducements now being held out by other islands, was referred to a committee. On the 26th of Dec. an Agricultural Show was held at Nisky, the country Moravian Station, under the auspices of the Humane Society.

It was the first ever held in the island, and proved a great success. Prizes were awarded to the exhibitors by His Excellency Governor Arendrup, who appeared to take a great interest in the proceedings.

On the 10th of Feb. 1891 His Excellency Governor Arendrup left for Europe for an absence of six months, and His Excellency Acting Vice-Governor Jürs, with family, arrived from St. Croix, and took up his abode in St. Thomas on 16th Feb. On the same evening there was a meeting of the Agricultural and Industrial Societies of St. Thomas, for the purpose of advancing the proposed Agricultural Show, which was to come off during the year.

On the 18th of August this Exhibition took place. It was held in town, and lasted two days, the first day being observed as a holiday. The Industrial exhibits were displayed in the Theatre, and the Agricultural in the Park adjoining. The ceremony of opening the Exhibition was entrusted to His Honour the Policemaster, H. M. W. Fischer, whose arrival was announced by the band playing the National Anthem.

He was received by the members of the committee, and introduced by the Rev. E. Foster, of Nisky, in a few appropriate words. His Honour then made a speech full of the interest he had for the island, and the hopes he had, that he might live to see the day when St. Thomas would be in cultivation from East to West, from North to South. He then declared the Exhibition opened.

An enormous crowd assisted and appreciated to their utmost both exhibits, which called for the highest praise from everyone on account of their variety. Almost every tropical production was represented, as well as specimens of Creole handicraft and Ladies' needlework. The display in the Theatre on the evening of the second day was extremely beautiful, and His Excellency Governor Arendrup and Mrs. Arendrup, arriving from Europe by the steamer at 9 p.m., and almost immediately after landing proceeding to the Exhibition, was such a graceful act, that they received an enthusiastic reception. The proceedings terminated with a street procession, marching to the music of a brass band, which ended what may be justly termed a red-letter day in the annals of St. Thomas, a day that showed in a striking manner what its inhabitants were capable of producing, and if the right stimulus were given, this "Island of the Sea" could be rendered as productive as when, 100 years ago, it was covered with flourishing estates.

It is unfortunate to chronicle, that with this energetic effort on the part of the Society its endeavours in this direction ceased. Acquiring the Estate "Crown," and parcelling out its land on favourable terms to the poorer class of agriculturists, it got involved in a law suit with its neighbours, which yet continues. Let us hope, with the settlement of this and the vexed question at issue, it may once more resume its labours and receive that encouragement which it truly deserves.

Reports were now being pretty extensively circulated of the probable transfer of St. Thomas to America. Nearly every mail from the United States brought newspapers containing articles, more or less, in favour of the project, notably the *New York Herald* and the *Sun*, which caused people to believe that sooner or later something would be done in the matter.

WASHING CLOTHES

PLAITING FISH POTS

But, like many a former rumour, it ended in nothing, though it was pretty generally felt, in the now rapidly increasing fortunes of the island, that a change of some sort would be beneficial. Prominent Americans believed that the acquisition of St. Thomas was desirable. Its harbour had been over and over again quoted by the best naval authorities as the finest in the West Indies. The American Government had coquetted with Haiti for the possession of Mole St. Nicolas, and with San Domingo, for the Bay of Samana, and had not succeeded in obtaining either of them. Here was a port ready made, as it were, with a harbour almost landlocked, capable of holding nearly 200 vessels, with a fine floating dock, wharves, large warehouses, a clean and well-kept town, substantial buildings, an intelligent and industrious people, in fact, everything most desirable for a Naval and Coaling Station. It was most natural that St. Thomas should receive attention in this respect. It is true, that America was just then on the verge of war with Chili, and felt the necessity of such a place, but with a peaceful settlement of the difficulty, the desire faded away, and Uncle Sam yet remains without a Naval Station in West Indian waters. Some fine day he will be caught napping, and then there will be some unpleasant hours at Washington.

On the 3rd of Nov. a telegram from St. Croix brought the news of the demise of Johan August Stakemann, K.D. and D.M., who retired from office in 1881. He was born in St. Thomas on the 14th of Dec. 1805. He was an accomplished scholar and jurist, a rare musician, and was one of the few natives who, by his abilities, had held on more than one occasion the reins of Government in both the islands.

In the month of December the Hon. Frederick A. Ober, Special Commissioner to the West Indies from the World's Columbian Exposition, arrived in St Thomas, to use his own words, "to obtain the co-operation of the Government in the Exposition." To this end he called upon His Excellency the Governor, Colonel Arendrup, who, unfortunately, was not at that time able to further his views. Appealing to the residents of the town, and being aware of the people's desire to make known their island as a winter resort, and its desirability as a Coaling Station, he recommended that, "a model or relief-map be prepared, showing the glorious harbour, the surrounding hills, the town, the tropical vegetation—in other words, a small exposition of the island, visible at a glance, that would convey to the world at large an adequate picture of its beauty and advantages." The idea was applauded by the Committee appointed to carry it into effect, and on Mr. Ober's second visit to St. Thomas, six weeks after, one of their number volunteered to reproduce the harbour, drawn to scale, and in such a shape as to be attractive to the general observer as well as valuable to the scientist.

On the 12th of Feb. 1892 a committee of gentlemen, presided over by His Excellency the Governor, was organized for the purpose of raising subscriptions towards Their Majesties', King Christian IX. and Queen Louise's, Golden Wedding Fund. On the 30th of March the 200th anniversary of the arrival of the military was observed by a display of flags from public as well as private places. On the 30th of April the Memorial to Their Majesties, the King and Queen of Denmark, on the occasion of their approaching Golden Wedding, from the Colonial Council, which had been entrusted to one of the members for execution, was forwarded, viâ St. Croix, to its destination. The papers of the day speak of it as an artistic production, creditable to all who took part in it. On the 28th of May the Golden Wedding of Their Majesties was observed by a large display of flags in town and harbour. At daylight a royal salute was fired, the various church bells ringing simultaneously. On the 20th of August a Draft of Ordinance prohibiting the circulation of money tokens was introduced into the Colonial Council. This was the first direct blow aimed at Mexican silver, which had now been in circulation for some years, causing serious loss and inconvenience to the people of St. Thomas. After the usual discussion the Draft was adopted, to be put in force about the middle of September.

On the 14th of Sept. the reign of Mexican silver came to an end. As the circulation of "tokens" was suppressed, the coal carriers struck work, and a mob of them invaded the town, carrying sticks and shouting to be paid in Danish money. After they had made loud demonstrations at the three steamship agencies, the crowd increasing at every moment and becoming more disorderly, a detachment of soldiers was ordered out to keep them in check. In the meanwhile, His Honour Policemaster Fischer and Police-Assistant Kjar strove to restore order. During the tumult most of the stores were closed; but when it became known that the Companies had agreed to pay their hands in Danish silver, it ceased almost as quickly as it had begun. It is the first time in the history of St. Thomas that the working class had been so near coming into conflict with the authority— for, as a rule, no more peaceable population exists in any community. It is more than probably due to the influence which Policemaster Fischer had over the more unruly of its members that nothing serious occurred.

The year 1893 opened with the demise of Secretary Hóther Hánschell, who for 18 years had faithfully served the Government, during which period he had earned the esteem of the public and all with whom he had been brought in contact officially or socially.

United States cruisers now began to drop into the harbour, and, with the French and German men-of-war, it presented an animated appearance. Splendid entertainments were given at Government House to the commanders and officers, who were likewise the recipients of much of that hospitality for which St. Thomas is famous.

On the 19th of Feb. the Pope's Golden Jubilee was celebrated by the members of the Catholic Congregation, who illuminated their houses and made a liberal display of bunting in honour of the occasion.

About this time a proposition was brought forward in the Colonial Council to establish a Mont de Pieté, or a Government pawnbroker's shop, where small loans on jewellery could be obtained at a moderate rate of interest. Unfortunately it was not in order, though, from what transpired, it appeared that an Ordinance to that effect had once been brought in and dropped, so that our "Island of the Sea" is yet a paradise for moneylenders, as much as five per cent. to ten per cent. per month being asked and given.

Since the opening of the year no less than 17 warships had anchored in the harbour, a strong proof of the appreciation by their Government of its advantages. England, Italy, Germany, and Russia were represented, and now several others were expected on their way to the Naval Review in New York, to celebrate the 300th anniversary of the discovery of America by Columbus. On the 11th of March six powerful men-of-war lay in the harbour, each representing a different nation. On the 12th the U.S. cruiser "Newark" arrived in port from Las Palmas, Canary Islands, with the caravel "Niña" in tow, and with her the U.S. cruiser "Bennington," towing the caravel "Pinta," *en route* for the World's Columbian Exposition. Boats filled with sightseers pulled off to see these facsimiles of the caravels in which Columbus sailed on his immortal voyage of discovery. Had it been possible to strip the scene of its modern accessories, one might have imagined the great navigator and his caravels once more in the harbour of St. Thomas, as he very likely was 400 years ago. Who knows if the Caribs who lived there then, did not look at these strange vessels with the same curiosity animating them, perhaps, that filled nearly every one in St. Thomas on the 12th of March 1893 at the sight of their counterparts?

It was an interesting event—and a day ever memorable in the annals of our "Island of the Sea." On the 1st of April the Port of St. Thomas was declared free, and the import dues raised three per cent. By this time the model of the island of St. Thomas was completed, and submitted to the Committee and the public of St. Thomas, who were so satisfied with its execution, that they determined to raise a subscription and send it to the World's Columbian Exposition, with Dr. C. E. Taylor, its constructor, and his son Clarence, who had assisted him. This was carried into effect, Dr. Taylor proceeding on the 23rd of April to America, and to the World's Fair, where he was officially recognized as Commissioner representing the island, and successfully installed it. Of its merits as a model, it was pronounced to be "worthy to stand alongside the best." It attracted general attention among the naval men connected with the Exposition, who remembered St. Thomas for the hospitality of its people, and as the finest harbour in the West Indies in which they had ever cast anchor. There was but one voice among all of them as to the desirability of our "Island of the Sea," as a Coaling Station for the United States of America. The model itself received many favourable notices from the Chicago Press, notably the *Tribune*. It was a miniature St. Thomas, the town, with over 1600 houses, and harbour with its ships, being faithfully pourtrayed. It even contained the American warships and the caravels. The country was also depicted with its ponds, watercourses, houses, roads, and estates.

MESSRS. BRONDSTED & CO.'S COAL WHARVES.

FACSIMILE OF CARAVEL.

It is gratifying to note that it gave great satisfaction to the Royal Danish Commission, and that Dr. Taylor was awarded the Medal and Diploma, his son Clarence receiving a handsome Certificate from the World's Fair Authorities, for having assisted him.

The commencement of this year was a busy one, no less than 48 steam vessels having called at St. Thomas during the month of March.

On the 2nd of May came the news of the death of Chamberlain Garde, formerly Governor of the Danish West Indies. The news was received with profound regret by many of his friends and the public.

"Under date of 15th May, the Governor of the Danish West Indies, Colonel C. H. Arendrup, C.D. and D.M., was, in virtue of his petition, granted his resignation from said office from 30th of June, account to reckon, with the notification of His Majesty the King's most high satisfaction with his work in that capacity."

On the 21st of June, at an Extraordinary Meeting of the Colonial Council, His Excellency rose to bid farewell to the Council on his retirement from the post of Governor. He referred gratefully to the services given by the officials; to the co-operation of the Honourable Council; to his relations with the Consular Body, as well as the clergymen of the different congregations. He spoke regretfully of the decline of trade, but hoped that the future of St. Thomas would be brighter, and wished every prosperity to the island and its inhabitants.

The Chairman called upon the Council to wish His Excellency a safe passage and success in his new sphere of labour, which was unanimously done, the members rising. His Excellency then shook hands with the Chairman, bowed to the members, and retired.

Thus passed from the public life of St. Thomas His Excellency Colonel Arendrup, who, during a trying time in its fortunes, had sustained the responsible post of Governor of these islands. It is too early yet to judge of his administration, which in times of adversity is always trying to men in high positions. But we are sure, that on all occasions His Excellency sought the welfare of these islands. Even in matters which related to individuals he acted conscientiously, always with kindness, but with unmistakeable firmness. He was a staunch friend—a lover of industrial and agricultural progress, and with an ever-decreasing Budget before him, always ready to effect what improvements it would allow. In private or official life he was always accessible, the poorest could gain admittance to him at any time and be patiently listened to: as host, everyone in St. Thomas, and those who have visited our "Island of the Sea," will remember the splendid entertainments given at Government House, where, with Madame Arendrup, he dispensed a hospitality which will be ever remembered.

His Excellency left the island on the 27th of June 1893, amidst cheering and a salute of 17 guns from the battery.

A heavy gale swept over the island on the 19th of August, doing considerable damage to the wharves; some roofing and spouting torn away, fences blown down, and trees torn up, were among the minor incidents.

On the 8th of Nov. His Excellency the Acting Vice-Governor Jürs took up his residence in St. Thomas.

His Excellency Colonel Carl Emil Hedemann, K.D., R.E., arrived on the 22nd of Dec., and, as Governor-General of the Danish West Indies, held an official reception at Government House, which was attended by the officials, members of Colonial Council, and many merchants and leading inhabitants of the island, who, after a sumptuous luncheon, departed most favourably impressed with the new Governor's courtesy and affability.

With the advent of the new Governor there is but little to chronicle of the year 1894.

On the 19th and 20th of July 1895 a picked eleven of cricketers from the island of St. Kitt's played against a picked eleven of St. Thomas. The former were victors. It was the first time that such a visit from a neighbouring island had taken place, and gave full scope for that hospitality and good feeling for which St. Thomas is famous.

The Silver Wedding of Their Royal Highnesses the Crown Prince Frederick and the Princess Louise was celebrated on the 28th of July with becoming loyalty. A subscription of 1087 dollars was collected, and an Address of Congratulation, elegantly illuminated, was forwarded.

The year 1895 saw the retirement of Policemaster H. M. W. Fischer, after 47 years' service in the Danish West Indies.

Born in the city of Flensburg in the year 1831, he volunteered for the war in 1848, and volunteered for the West Indies in the latter part of that year, when a force of 400 men was dispatched from the army in order to quell the insurrection of the slaves in St. Croix in that year. Arriving in that island, and finding it quelled, they requested to be sent home again to take part in the war, sending a petition to the Home Government to that effect. Being detained, Mr. Fischer served in his regiment until employed in Government office as writer, with the rank of sergeant. In 1857 he was constituted as royal clerk, and as such removed to St. Thomas, in the then office of the Presidency, in the month of February 1859. On the 1st of April 1861 he was nominated Assistant-Policemaster in St. Thomas, and on the 12th of June 1871 Acting Policemaster until the 20th of April 1873, when he received royal appointment as such. On the 7th of Oct. 1881 he was made a Knight of Dannebrog.

We have seen, in the course of this history, how on all occasions the services of Policemaster Fischer were appreciated by the people of these islands. It may be said of him that, with the exception of His Excellency the Governor, few officials, and these islands can boast of many good ones, ever had the interests and welfare of the people more at heart than himself. A long acquaintance with their manners and customs fully qualified him for the post which he so faithfully filled for so many years in St. Thomas. To say that he were faultless, would be to make him more than human. This, I am sure, he never pretended to be; but that he did his duty conscientiously and fearlessly is written on the pages of his life from the beginning of his career in the West Indies to the end of it. For this, on his retirement, the inhabitants of St. Thomas, through a Committee of prominent citizens, presented him with a gold medal, an illuminated address, in a box of native manufacture, and a piece of silver, which was handed to him some time after his arrival in Copenhagen, for which city he left St. Thomas, with his estimable wife, viâ the United States of America, on the 13th of August. Such a tribute from the Danish West Indian people had never before been given to a Danish official.

With this episode I conclude my historical sketch, referring my readers to the following pages for a review of the present condition of our "Island of the Sea."

PART II.

THE PRESENT.

AND now that we have gone through the pages of its history, let us take a look as it is to-day.

We have traced it from the time when the first naked Caribs trod its shores, living in rude huts and earning a precarious livelihood by hunting and fishing. We have seen it, from a mere handful of adventurers, become the centre of a commerce almost unparalleled in the West Indies. We have seen it the resort of pirates and buccaneers, and a rendezvous for convoys of merchant vessels, and for individuals of every nationality under the sun. We have seen it passing from the iron-handed rule of a Jörgen Iwersen to that of successive Governors, all vested with more or less extraordinary powers; with its harbour crowded with sailing vessels, and its streets crowded with purchasers; its hills cultivated almost to their summits, and its fertile valleys full of tropical products; with disease and pestilence at its doors, or rendered a desolate waste from the hurricane and earthquake. We have seen it in such good fortune as has fallen to the lot of few islands in these seas. We are now to behold it with its magnificent harbour and improvements, its great coaling facilities, its wharves and Floating Dock, capable of receiving steamers and large vessels of over 3000 tons, its Marine slip and railway for the repairing of smaller craft, its immense cisterns for the storage of water for the supply of vessels, its Factory, where nearly every conceivable kind of ironwork for the repair of steamships can be turned out, where a shaft or boiler can be made, or a propeller repaired or iron launches built, its stevedores' service for the loading and discharging of vessels, its telegraph station, its hospitals, its medical staff, its Ice-house, its contractors for ships' supplies, its ship carpenters and caulkers, its well-built city, its polite officials, its mild and good Government, its civilized and industrious inhabitants; and though shorn of its ancient prosperity, yet worthy indeed of the name I have given it, "An Island of the Sea."

ST. THOMAS.

MAIN STREET.

And I am not the only one who grows enthusiastic over it. Scarcely anybody who visits its shores, but what goes away pleased with the place and the people. Hear what Mr. F. Ober says of it *:—

"As daylight comes, it is seen what a beautiful harbour is this of St. Thomas, worthy of all the adjectives one can heap upon it, magnificent, gem-like, glorious. Hills on all sides surround it, save towards the southern sea, where the entrance lies between two high promontories, guarded by ancient forts. Hills behind it, sunburnt and bare, look down upon a charming town, itself built upon three elevations, and one of the most picturesque places in the Caribbean Sea. One rarely hears the name of this town, the port of St. Thomas, but it is called Charlotte Amalia, and is a good old-fashioned settlement, clean and pretty, with straight streets, good wharves, street and harbour lights, a fine police force, a stable Government and most delightful situation. There is not another like it anywhere for comfort and convenience, and it fitly supplements the advantages of its royal harbour as a place of call, and even detention, for the naval vessels cruising in those seas."

I quote thus extensively from one of America's best-informed writers on West Indian topics, to show what an impression this "Island of the Sea" made upon him, and were I not afraid of wearying my readers, I could fill these pages with quotations from the *New York Herald*, the *Sun*, and *Detroit Free Press*, all containing articles in a similar strain; so different to those of prejudiced writers, who may have never seen the place, or who had their own petty interest to serve. There is no need to add to the description of Mr. Ober, which, for picturesqueness and accuracy, stands unrivalled; but there are so many points of vantage from which to view our "Island of the Sea," that I may well be pardoned if I sketch a few of them. Are you a stranger and desirous of seeing it under different aspects? Take a walk up any one of the hills which lead to Bluebeard's or Blackbeard's Castle; if their owners kindly permit you to inspect them, mount to the top of either of these ancient buildings.

What a sight lies below you! The bay is crowded with vessels. The red-roofed houses lie snugly at the foot of the

---

* "In the Wake of Columbus."

hill, little clumps of bananas and cocoa palms standing out in relief. Far away to the south is St. Croix, to the west Porto Rico, their dim and hazy outlines scarcely visible on the dark blue sea. Buck Island is not far off, and Frenchman's Cap, a rugged rock, whose base, white with the foam of the turbulent element surrounding it, stands solitary amidst the waste of waters. Estate Thomas, Havensigt, and the Lazaretto are to the left. All dainty spots to look at, full of flowers and tropical foliage. To right and left are islets with sandy bays, fringed with the seaside grape or wild mangrove. Within are the coal wharves of the different companies. Between what is called the Haul-over, you may get a glimpse of Water Island, and to the right of the passage which has been cut through it, and which has done so much for the sanitation of the harbour, you will see "Villa Olga," a tastefully appointed residence, whose interior is a perfect cabinet of bric-a-brac and art treasures, situated on one of the most lovely spots on the island; and what a garden adjoins it, what a wealth of rose trees and flowers! Bananas and pine apples, mangoes, and fruit trees of every description. Cosy nooks with seats in them, pleasant walks and shady places, and a serpentine road leading you to the top of a mountain, which when reached will give you, from its pavilion, a view of such surpassing grandeur and beauty, that you will wonder that you had never heard of it before.

It is a sight one does not easily forget, in years afterwards, is this town of St. Thomas, as seen through the windows of the charming dwelling I have mentioned, extending to the left of you, with cocoa-nut palms waving in the foreground, the busy harbour with its shipping, and Bluebeard's Castle melting away, as it were, in the haze of the distance.

Then, if you care to climb the hills again, till you reach Louisenhoi, and, standing on the summit, you look down on the town, as we have described it, below, and on the other side of the island, Magen's Bay, where its translucent waters, of an emerald green, plash eternally upon a sandy shore of snowy whiteness. A scene such as few pens can describe—certainly not mine. Now descend we from the picturesque to the prosaic, if it were possible to be so, in describing Charlotte Amalia.

The town itself is essentially a business place, as its merchants are thoroughgoing business men. Its great commercial houses

VILLA OLGA...

of yore may have departed, but those that remain are fully alive to the exigencies of the situation. They know that St. Thomas is no longer the Emporium of the Antilles, but they have very sensibly gone to work and improved their town and harbour—their harbour especially.

In the first place, they have made it free—free to come in and free to go out—for vessels seeking, and this, at a cost to themselves of one per cent. extra, paid on their duties, making three per cent. instead of two per cent., as formerly. Then, again, they have managed to cheapen everything, as it never was before.

You can coal cheaper, telegraph cheaper, repair vessels cheaper, and water vessels cheaper, and with better water than elsewhere in the West Indies. These are facts which can be proved by reference to important papers on the subject. Then, again, they have provided a Lazaretto, where those who are quarantined in it, pass a happy and pleasant time with an educated and intelligent Inspector and his family, amidst such agreeable surroundings, that we have it actually on record that some persons have regretted to leave it. Then, again, the sanitary condition of the town has been so vastly improved, that, according to the testimony of our able and esteemed King's Physican, Dr. Mortensen, our death rate will compare favourably with most places in the civilized world. A more cleanly town to-day than Charlotte Amalia scarcely exists. From the trimly-kept Fort, used as a Prison and Police Station, and the handsomely-built Barracks, down to the smallest building, you will be struck with the air of cleanliness which prevails. All the streets are macadamized, with gutters at each side of them paved with stone. The three principal water courses, or "Guts," as they are called, are paved in the same manner, and carry down the water from the mountains to the sea.

The stores are massive, brick built, extend to the water's edge some 400 feet, have iron tracks running alongside of them for the carriage of goods, and are solidity itself. There are probably 100 such, built, many of them, at a cost of 50,000 dollars to 60,000 dollars apiece. Each has its wharf for the landing of goods, and some of them powerful cranes to hoist them up. It is sad to compare their present inactivity with the life of former days, when work in them commenced at

5 a.m., heads of the firm and their clerks being at their posts together, especially in the busy season. If it be different to-day, it is because the maddening rush for wealth is over, and men no longer expect to make a fortune in a few years to go to Europe and spend it. Thus you will see that merchants take things easier and come down, between 7 and 9 a.m., some of them in cabs, so perfect a picture of contentment, that a Wall Street millionaire might justly envy them. Do not suppose by this, that any of them sit with their hands folded when they get to work. There is yet business enough left in our "Island of the Sea" to keep nearly everyone occupied until 5 or 6 p.m., when the stores close, and they all go home for dinner. And this, as those who have partaken of West Indian hospitality, is almost always an enjoyable affair. People live well in St. Thomas as a rule, and to these fresh from the rough fare of ship board, or a tour in the interior of San Domingo, Hayti, or Porto Rico, the clean, snowy tablecloth, the polished silver, and the neat appointments of a St. Thomas breakfast or dinner table, are something to be remembered.

This brings me to our accommodations for passengers. True, there are no hotels on the European nor American plan. There is, indeed, nothing imposing in that direction; but there is the Hotel du Commerce, a place that has existed for many years. It fronts the harbour, close to the landing-place and the Emancipation Garden, and, if not too fastidious, one can be very happy and comfortable for the days he may have to spend there. Then there are private boarding-houses of different grades. One or two of them elegantly furnished, where the scent of countless roses greets you in the early morn through your window, and where you may enjoy everything of the best that can be found in a West Indian home. And society will not be found wanting, for in the months of December, January, February, and March, when the harbour is crowded with vessels, and ships of war come in, to wake you in the morn with the boom of cannon saluting the old brick Fort, you may participate in a round of gaiety almost bewildering to the lover of repose. His Excellency the Governor then resides in St. Thomas, and the doors of Government House, a splendid building, handsomely decorated and well appointed, are thrown open, dancing and dinner parties succeeding each other, until one wonders how human nature can stand so much, with the thermometer sometimes at 80.

KING'S WHARF.

That the ladies—and there are many of them young and beautiful—do so, seemingly as fresh as ever at each entertainment, is positive; and so the ball rolls merrily on until the busy season becomes dull again, and the hurricane months set in, a period that extends from 25th July to 25th Oct.; the bê'e noir of every one, and a time when the harbour is empty, streets are empty, and, as a consequence, pockets are empty. Yet the people bear it manfully, thankful if they pull through without one of those storms for which the West Indies are famous, and which, once experienced, leave a nameless dread behind them.

But soon the Christmas season comes along; the stores are gay with merchandize, toys and presents are liberally displayed, Christmas cards and gifts are bought in wild profusion, for with business once again revived and money floating freely, past cares are all forgotten.

And in the harbour a like activity prevails; the boatman finds a harvest among the tourists, who, to escape the chilly blasts of northern winters, come to these climes for health and recreation. The naked urchins who go alongside the steamers which bring these friendly visitors pick up many a sixpence by diving after them in the water. Vendors of curios, sea-shells, branches of coral white as snow, and tropical fruits, are also there for the purpose of selling them to the passengers. Boats pass to and from the men-of-war and King's wharf, sometimes conveying officers dressed in uniform to pay visits to their entertainers of the night before, or perhaps a party of ladies and gentlemen to breakfast or dine with some foreign admiral, if in port. Truly, the interchange of civilities is never-ending, and long remembered afterwards by the recipients. I have talked with naval officers at the World's Fair, Chicago, who have remembered with delight the hospitality of St. Thomas. And when a large party of tourists are leaving the island, the landing-place is a sight to look at, so encumbered is it with their purchases. Piles of boxes of bay rum, for the production of which the island is famous, Florida water,* which is made here of surpassing excellence, and wines, liqueurs, preserves, and pickles, all of which are to be obtained cheap and of very good

---

* Mr. H. Michelsen makes a superior quality of bay rum and Florida water, so does our esteemed apothecary, Mr. A. H. Rüse. Both these gentlemen were awarded the Medal and Diploma at the World's Columbian Exposition.

quality, lay strewn upon the wharf, with here and there a package or two of genuine Havana cigars. This bustle and life extends to all parts of the water's edge in this season of the island's activity; from the fishwomen who sell the fish that the men have caught in their fish-pots overnight, to the women who coal the steamers at Messrs. Bröndsted and Company's great coal wharves, all are constantly employed. Busy as bees are the coal-women when at this exhausting labour; hundreds of them, each with a basket of coal on her head, run along the gangway leading to the steamer, empty it, and run back to have it once again refilled. Most striking is this scene at midnight, when they sing songs in a quaint minor key, never ceasing their labour until the huge steamer is properly coaled; then the *flambeaux* which have lighted up coals, women, overseers, and officers of the ship go out, and all is quiet once more.

All this movement may seem incredible to those who have been accustomed to associate life in the tropics with laziness and a disinclination to exertion, especially where the negroes are concerned; give them work, and pay them properly for it, and they will do it quite as promptly, and far more good-naturedly, than their white brother in a like station of life, who, the slave perhaps of some trade union, is far worse off to-day than the negro ever was at the time of slavery.

A number of large steamers coal at Messrs. Bröndsted and Company's wharf every month; from eight to ten thousand tons of coal may be found piled up in a stack at a time. I have heard it said by steamship captains that this firm can coal a steamer faster and cheaper than any other in the West Indies.

There is a natural dry dock, just between the German Company's wharf and that of Messrs. Bröndsted and Company; as if Nature had predestined St. Thomas to be the future Naval Station of such a power as America, there is a cove, oblong in shape, only requiring a pair of gates to make it the most perfect and commodious dry dock in the West Indies. If we add to this, that an arsenal and store-houses could be built alongside its shores, properly sheltered from an enemy's shot or shell in case of an attack— I think, I have shown pretty conclusively the immense natural advantages which the harbour of St. Thomas possesses above all others in the West Indies—it could be made impregnable. In this I am supported by more than one authority in such matters.

Now let me get back to town again. I have had, in the course of the island's history, to tell of disease and pestilence, hurricane and earthquake. The former, owing to greatly improved sanitation, no longer exists, and the latter so rarely visits our "Island of the Sea," that people hardly take them into account unless very severe, which is but rarely.

Hurricanes are certainly unpleasant visitors, as, indeed, are all such natural phenomena; but with a fall in the barometer, indicating its approach, people make ready for it, and as the houses are built pretty strongly, few of them are blown away bodily, as in the great tornadoes which are common in America, unless the "blow" be an unusually severe one.

To feel the ground trembling under you is also an unpleasant visitation; but as such earthquakes as that of 1867 only occur once in 300 years, it will be seen that St. Thomas is singularly free from them—at least those of a really destructive character. With regard to the frequency of hurricanes, St. Thomas has only been visited by them ten times in a period covering 397 years, out of nearly 140 hurricanes and severe gales which have committed more or less injury in the West Indies. They undoubtedly do a great deal of damage to fences, crops, and the smaller wooden tenements, unroofing houses, and wrecking vessels in the harbour, should its violence be sufficient to cause them to break away from their anchorage; but, as if in compensation, the seasons become more regular, rains fall with greater frequency, and the climate becomes more equable. And it is wonderful how soon the people begin to clear away the wreckage and recover from the disaster; so quickly, that it would seem as if no such thing had happened. Who would believe, looking at St. Thomas to-day, that a hurricane or tidal wave had ever devastated it? To my mind, and I have in the course of my early travels witnessed both, a blizzard or a tornado such as can sweep away half a city in a few minutes in America, are far more formidable visitants. Change their names to hurricane or cyclone, and I think Uncle Sam can beat the West Indies hollow in such matters.

English is the language generally spoken; it might be said to be the language of the country if Danish were not the official. Spanish, French, and German are also spoken by many of the inhabitants; but as the commerce with the Spanish Colonies has decreased, the young men no longer seek to acquire the Spanish language. With a liberality not usual among Continental nations, Denmark never extended compulsory military service to the Colonies. There were volunteer corps once on a time, which turned out now and then with all the "pomp and circumstance of war," but none of them remain except the Brand Corps, which is actually the Fire Brigade, under a brand-major and officers; this is very effective and does its duty well, and when assisted by the coal and other women, who, when the cry of fire is raised, rush to the scene with their buckets full of water, will stay a conflagration quicker than those with better appliances.

Nor did Denmark ever offer to enforce the compulsory acquirement of Danish. It may be said our "Island of the Sea" has actually as liberal a Government as any under the sun. There is one newspaper, the *St. Thomas Tidende*; the *Bulletin* and *Mail Notes* are dailies; they have a fair circulation, and are filled with many items of local interest to their subscribers.

There is a Colonial Council, elected by the people; a Reconciling Court, which, bringing plaintiff and defendant together before two citizen judges, and reconciling them, when possible, saves endless suits at law; a Town Court tries criminal cases. There is no trial by jury, but the judges are men of probity, and it is quite sure that a man stands just as good a chance of a fair trial before the one man as he would before "twelve men, good and true." There is a Special Court, which may be held any day, and a Dealing Court; this investigates the circumstances of all deceased persons, sees that wills are properly executed, administers to the affairs of all who die intestate, and takes charge of all assets in cases of bankruptcy on behalf of creditors. Imprisonment for debt is yet in vogue; but as the unfortunate creditor has to feed his debtor, it seems rather hard, especially as, should the creditor fail to send the money for his debtor's maintenance, he walks out a free man, and he cannot imprison him again for the debt. There are many other institutions, charitable and otherwise—a Humane Society, a Home for Destitute Children—all testifying to the advanced condition of the people.

Compulsory vaccination exists, but many parents pay the fine in preference to running the ghastly risk of arm-to-arm vaccination, whereby leprosy has, on more than one occasion, been

DWELLING HOUSE, LAZARETTO.

LAZARETTO

transmitted. It must be said, however, that the law is very severe on any careless physician, and that the utmost care is observed. There is also compulsory education; the private schools are good, but a College is sadly needed for the higher education of both sexes, who are eager to learn and are not deficient in natural ability.

There are several churches; the Lutheran, which is the State Church, the Roman Catholic, Moravian, Episcopalian, Dutch Reformed, and Methodists. The Israelites have a pretty synagogue, which in past days was always filled with a large and influential congregation. One can pass a pleasant Sunday in St. Thomas: the Danes are far from straight-laced, and can tolerate a little music and honest pleasure after church hours. A man may open his store before 9 a.m. and open it again at 4 p.m.: few do this, though the thirsty traveller has no need to slink through the back door to get a drink, as is the case in some other cities, and a good cigar is as obtainable on the Lord's day as any other. The population of St. Thomas is not so large as in former days—about 12,000 in town or country; it is mixed, all shades of complexion being the rule. A better dressed or more orderly cannot be found anywhere; a glance at its streets on Sundays especially will prove this. The Madras head kerchief is fast disappearing; gaudy jewellery and loud colours are the exceptions. Hats of all shapes and fashion are worn by the women and neat prints and delainettes. Nearly everyone can read and write, and with but few exceptions sobriety is prevalent. Music and dancing are much in vogue, and pleasant parties are given by all classes.

Much has been written of the immorality prevalent in the West Indies; but with an experience of 30 years in them, I can safely say that they are virtue personified by the sides of London, Chicago, Paris, and New York.

The West Indian of any colour is the best-hearted and most hospitable soul alive: he is eminently charitable, even when he has to share his meal with a starving fellow-creature; he is cleanly too: he takes his "tub" in the morning regularly, and his wife, if he be a poor man, takes good care to keep him in a clean shirt and clothes; the women make the best of wives. Unfortunately, the young men are obliged to leave the island in search of remunerative employment; this leaves the colony with many young ladies yet waiting for husbands; they excel as housekeepers; and some of them have stores on the main street, which they manage successfully—at any rate, never become bankrupt. A good deal of private selling is done by respectable people; who pay a license for a "seller," one dollar per month, and importing small indents of goods, do a business this way which is often remunerative, as they have no taxes to pay. There are few places of amusement; a travelling company may visit the island now and again, when the Apollo Theatre is a scene of gaiety and amusement. Amateur theatricals and cantatas are got up for benevolent purposes.

Life is only dull in the hurricane season, and then it is sometimes too warm to do anything with actual pleasure; though, from the situation of the island, cool and invigorating breezes sweep over it at night.

There are two Banks, the St. Thomas and the Colonial. There is also a Savings Bank, a Public Library (the Athenæum), cafés, and refreshment saloons. Living is not too expensive; but one can live well or economically as his means will allow him. St. Thomas imports many nice things to tempt the epicure, and dinner parties are given at times of which Lucullus himself might be envious.

There are several lines of steamers which call at St. Thomas regularly, in fact, more steamers call at this island than there ever did before in its palmiest days, and it is to this facility of intercourse by direct communication that St. Thomas owes the loss of much of its commercial importance. Every island in the West Indies, every spot on the Spanish Main, which used to send its purchasers and its produce to our "Island of the Sea" now does so direct, steamers calling almost at their doors for them. On the other hand, this influx of vessels of large tonnage brings money to the port in various ways, besides giving employment to a number of people. The Hamburg Steamship Company alone has 15 steamers calling monthly, the Compagnie Générale Transatlantique four, the Royal Mail Steamship Company two, besides cargo boats; then there are the Quebec Line and others of considerable importance.

It is reasonable to believe that were there not such a depression existing all over the West Indies on account of the low prices of sugar, a striking improvement would take place in the shipping business of St. Thomas. It is well known that old abuses have been swept away, that its port is free,

A ROYAL VISIT.

On the 22nd December 1895, His Royal Highness Prince Carl of Denmark arrived in St. Thomas, on board H.M.S. Fyen, Captain Caroe. Shortly after anchoring, His Excellency Governor Hedemann went off to the ship and was received under a salute of fifteen guns. There was a reception at Government House that evening at which His Royal Highness was present.

The Official landing did not take place till next day, when, precisely at three o'clock p.m., His Royal Highness came on shore accompanied by Commander Caroe. He was received by His Excellency Governor Hedemann and a guard of honour, consisting of the 2nd Company of the West Indian Regiment under the command of Captain Paludan. A number of Officials, Consuls, and Members of the Colonial Council were presented by the Governor to His Royal Highness, who cordially shook hands with each one of them.

Prince Carl then entered the Governor's carriage and drove off to Government House amidst the hearty applause of the people, hundreds of whom lined the King's Wharf and its approaches. The Prince was attired in the uniform of a Naval Lieutenant, wearing in addition the broad blue sash of the Order of the Elephant.

A little later he drove through the town, much to the gratification of the populace. In the evening, there was a Reception and a Dance at Government House.

On the 15th January 1896, H.M.S. Fyen proceeded to St. Croix, where H.R.H. Prince Carl was enthusiastically welcomed. After spending a few days in that beautiful island, in which a round of Festivities succeeded his arrival, His Royal Highness returned to St. Thomas, on board H.M.S. Fyen, on the 28th January, and left for Europe on the 2nd of February, followed by the good wishes of everyone who had been brought in contact with him publicly or privately.

He was the second Danish Prince who had ever trod West Indian soil, and like his uncle, H.R.H. Prince Valdemar, whose memory is yet green among some of the older inhabitants, was received with such demonstrations of loyalty and affection as to impress him with the love and devotion that the people of these islands have always maintained towards the Royal House of Denmark.

and that no more desirable harbour can be found anywhere in these waters. One can but hope that a change may come shortly, a better state of affairs for the whole of the West Indies, for with it must come an improved condition of things for St. Thomas.

And now I would like to say a few words about the country, and what its soil is capable of producing. The island itself is situated in lat. 18° 20′ 42″ N. and long. 64° 48′ 9″ W.; its length is about 13 miles east and west, with an average breadth of three miles; its appearance is that of a range of high dome-shaped hills, running from west to east. These reach an elevation of 1515 English feet towards the western part, and make a striking picture when looked at by a stranger arriving for the first time from Europe or America.

The country roads are few, and as might be expected from the nature of the island, which is mountainous; but pleasant drives in any of the numerous cabs may be had to Smith's Bay or John Bruce's Bay. As I have already written, no more fertile or romantic spots can be found in the West Indies than among its hills and valleys. If the estates are not cultivated, it must not be forgotten that slavery, with its usual train of evils, is the cause; for no sooner was freedom proclaimed in the year 1848, than the slaves flocked into town, sought more lucrative employment among the shipping, and places which had heretofore yielded handsome revenues to their owners fell to rack and ruin in consequence. The very name of agriculture was hateful to the slave, and the spade and the hoe but badges of a detestable servitude, which always recalled it to his memory when he looked at them.

It has required years to eradicate this feeling, but now that compulsory education is beginning to exert its sway—and you cannot find more apt scholars than many of the coloured children at the public schools—their eyes are being opened; they are beginning to understand that in that same soil there is a mine of wealth, or at least enough to secure them an honest independence: and our black brothers in St. Thomas to-day are once more turning to the cultivation of small holdings which, by easy payments, become in a short time their own.

An Agricultural Society formed of influential gentlemen, merchants, and planters, looks after the important scheme, and from the success which has attended its efforts hitherto, by-and-by we shall find St. Thomas once again in cultivation.

Fruits and vegetables of all kinds are grown here. Coffee of an excellent quality; also tobacco can be raised. They were so, in large quantities, by the early settlers, why can it not be done again? One has only to look at the island as it was 100 years ago to answer that question. As far back as 1775 there were 69 plantations, 27 of which were of sugar cane, the rest being devoted to the raising of stock cotton, tobacco, and other produce. In 1792 there were 74 plantations, 40 in cane, and 34 in cotton; hence, we may infer that St. Thomas was not only commercially prosperous in former days, but remarkably so as an agricultural community. And now come up with me in the mountains, and I will show you bits of colour and places clothed with such beautiful verdure, and such a variety of ferns, creepers, and shrubs, that you have rarely seen before outside of these islands. On all sides will you see wonders of Nature's own providing. Here a broad gut or gully, down which a tiny stream of water is trickling musically among the rocks; it is overhung with trees of several kinds. There, the morning glory and acacia bend low with last night's showers; birds, few in species, but many in number, burst out into song; tamarinds, palms, and soursops (*Anona muricata*), grow here with others, as the sugar apple (*Anona squamosa*); and in wild profusion trees and vines are hidden beneath thousands of air plants and parasites, which are the most conspicuous vegetation. A lizard runs out and looks curiously at you, as you step upon a twig which crackles under your feet. You look below upon the little town whose busy hum no longer greets your ears; the sea looks like glass, and is dotted here and there with many a sail which seem as specks upon the water; hill and valley, luxuriant in tropical foliage, roll beneath you; the shore lines are broken, huge rocks stand out grey and bare, alternated by lovely bays; fleecy clouds float airily along, casting their shadows upon the land, changing its aspect at every moment; but the noontide sun now warns you to descend. You do so lingeringly, and resolving that future walks like these, to other spots as beautiful, shall not be left untried while you are a sojourner at St. Thomas. This is the picturesque side, now let us contemplate it from one more practical.

COMMUNAL HOSPITAL.

MILITARY HOSPITAL.

Baron Eggers, author of a valuable work on the flora of these islands, published under the auspices of the Smithsonian Institute, Washington, says, in 1883, "that a new era of industry would open up in St. Thomas, if it were made to bear products which would have not only a local value but also could be exported and disposed of in the world's markets. The palatable guinea corn (*Sorghum*), which grows here with astonishing luxuriance, could to a great extent replace the now generally used corn meal."

"Coffee can also be produced, as well as an endless variety of vegetables and tropical fruits. The large areas, which at present give no return could, however, so far as they cannot be used for the cultivation of vegetables or as pastures, be made at least as profitable as the more fertile areas which are now used for other purposes, and that without requiring so much capital to do so."

"On these worthless stretches of land the valuable product known as divi-divi (*Lebidibia coriaria*), which is found growing wild in all the islands, mostly in St. Thomas, can be grown in large quantities, and as this article is worth from 60 dollars to 70 dollars per ton, and the cost of cultivation is small, it would pay owners of such tracts of land to raise it, and if the tannin could be extracted from it on the spot, the cost of freight being saved, there would, in a short time, be a valuable article of export available."

"Of the fibre-producing plants there is the agave, which grows wild in great numbers everywhere in the island, often upon the naked rocks. The plant attains an immense size—the individual leaves often being over eight feet long by one foot broad, and weighing over 50 pounds; these leaves contain a countless number of fine, strong fibres, which make up eight to ten per cent. of the total weight, and in strength and appearance are equal to the best Manilla hemp, which they surpass in durability under water; the value of its fibre in England is £30 to £40 per ton."

It is not within the limits of this work to speak of all the valuable plants which this eminent botanist enumerates as growing upon the island of St. Thomas, and which by proper cultivation and the employment of capital, could be made the source of large and profitable incomes. It is sufficient to mention the bark of the seaside grape (*Coccoloba*), the bark of the mangrove (*Rhizophora*), as other tannin-producing trees growing here; and of the fibre-producing varieties, a plant of the pine apple (*Pitcairnia*), the wild growing pinguin (*Bromelia Pinguin*), several species of *Corchorus*, from which jute is manufactured, the guanatail (*Sanseviera guineensis*), the commercial value of which is about 250 dollars per ton; the cocoa palm, the wild horseradish (*Moringa*), the seeds of which contain a fine oil which never become rancid, the castor oil plant, the well-known aloe, which grows wild and could easily be planted on a large scale, not to speak of a variety of plants and spices of great commercial value, and into the detail of which space precludes our going.

Thus far we have sketched the present of St. Thomas, of its future it were as hazardous to speak as it would be of the most prosperous of the West Indies as they are to-day. It seems difficult to believe that their race is run, any more than it is to conceive of such a port as St. Thomas being deserted. There is no knowing what the whirligig of time may produce. More than 200 years ago Charlotte Amalia was ruined and almost abandoned, and yet it became prosperous to an extent never known before.

Let us hope, then, with greater advantages, an intelligent population, and every facility for the vessels which call there, no port in these waters will be more popular than that of St. Thomas, no people more prosperous than those who live in "An Island of the Sea."

PART III.

SHORT STORIES

ABOUT

BLUEBEARD'S

AND

BLACKBEARD'S CASTLES.

BLUEBEARD'S CASTLE.

"BLUEBEARD'S CASKET."

A LEGEND OF ST. THOMAS, DANISH WEST INDIES.

CHAPTER I.

THERE are few of us who have not heard the story of Bluebeard, that grim old Oriental tyrant who, after consigning so many wives to a violent death for their fatal curiosity, was at last slain himself by the brothers of Fatima.

But there are very few, indeed, who have read the story of his West Indian prototype, who, some years ago paid periodical visits to St. Thomas, in the Danish West Indies, leaving behind him at the end of his career a record beside which the original Bluebeard might pose as a saint and a martyr.

Commanding a schooner, whose beautiful lines and rakish look betokened her unlawful calling, and whose small draft of water enabled her to sail in such shallow depths that no sloop-of-war of those days could follow her, Bluebeard had made himself famous. Ostensibly a trader between the islands, he in reality trafficked in slaves, and not a few deeds of piracy might have been laid at his door.

But it is in the island of St. Thomas where he was best known, and this, too, among that portion of the population—the feminine—which then, as it is now, was in the majority. Whether it was on account of his handsome face, agreeable conversation, or lavish expenditure I am not able to tell you; certain it is that after a few moments spent in his company you were left with the impression that a more charming personage had never addressed you, and that all the stories you had ever heard to his disparagement, and these were legion among a certain portion of the community, could only be the offspring of envy. Thus it was, that whenever this redoubtable pirate came in contact with those who were not of the clique which claimed to know him so thoroughly, they never believed the horrible stories afloat concerning the atrocities he had committed, and he was a welcome guest at most of their houses.

It must, however, be remembered that in those days society in the West Indies was not quite so respectable as it is at present and in a place like St. Thomas, whose harbour contained, year in and year out, from one to 200 vessels of all nationalities, it could hardly be expected to be otherwise, more especially as from the hospitable nature of its people as well as from motives of business, they invited the captains freely to their homes, and hob-nobbed and dined with the veriest strangers, often. I am sorry to state, to their own disadvantage—as the history of many a broken heart of many a fair lady might tell you—for the gentle sex then was just as susceptible to a pair of epaulettes, a cocked hat and sword, as they are to-day; and as Bluebeard wore all of them, besides a pair of pistols stuck in his waistband, he was the recipient of many favours from the public, not to speak of the ladies of St. Thomas.

But the principal element in the liking which most of them had for Bluebeard was, undoubtedly, curiosity. Just as Fatima risked her life to gain a knowledge of the secret chamber, so these ladies would willingly have risked theirs to have gained a knowledge of the inner life of the handsome pirate who had enslaved them with his killing glances and his costly presents of silken gear and jewellery; for his was a generous hand, and he was lavish in his gifts to anyone who caught his fancy.

"As well he might be," often remarked his detractors, "seeing how easily he has come by them," though of this they had not an atom of proof beyond hearsay, for no witness had as yet turned up to tell the story of Bluebeard's piracy, "because," as these envious people would again remark, "neither vessel nor passengers have been spared to do so"; Bluebeard, according to their account, sinking the former, and making the latter walk the plank to get rid of them, such sailors who refused to join his bloodthirsty crew, sharing the same miserable fate.

And yet this self-same crew compared favourably with that of any other vessel in the harbour. If some of them did have a villainous look, and others were not quite so refined as they might have been when they got on a long shore cruise, they always dressed neatly and spoke civilly to everyone with whom they came in contact; besides, they had plenty of money, which they spent freely, and this goes a long way with some people, especially in a seaport like St. Thomas, where it is natural that everyone living more or less by the flotsam and jetsam of the sea that comes to it, must naturally respect the hand which doles out cheerfully the wherewithal to pay its footing.

What if dark stories were told about Bluebeard and his crew and his rakish-looking schooner, was not St. Thomas a free port to all nations? If the Captain of H.M.S. of war "Bulldog," who on more than one occasion had been detailed to watch Bluebeard, had not been able to catch him in any flagrant act of piracy on the high seas, why should those who were the recipients of his bounty be overscrupulous?

Thus it was that Bluebeard, at the time our story opens, was a welcome guest at St. Thomas, a favourite with both sexes, especially the ladies—I might add as great an enigma to their husbands as he was an object of curiosity to themselves. I have never been able to learn very positively how it was that Bluebeard became the possessor of the tower to the east of Charlotte Amalia, the one pretty little town of which St. Thomas can boast. From some letters which came into my possession a few years ago I have every reason to believe that he purchased it, with the town adjoining, for a very large sum of money. These letters also speak of a most lovely young woman, a Creole of the island, so superior in all that constituted beauty and excellence, that Bluebeard fell madly in love with her at first sight, and swore within himself that she should shortly belong to him. Perhaps this was the reason why he became the purchaser of the old tower, which is now named after him, and was so willing to pay so much more than its value. Don Geronimo Cordoban, the proprietor of it, and the father of the beautiful girl we have mentioned, being in great pecuniary difficulties at the time, Bluebeard, no doubt, may have thought it a stroke of policy to place him under some obligation by paying so liberally for it in order to secure the entrance to Don Geronimo's mansion, which was situated on the road below the tower, or Castle, as it was more generally termed, and was not many minutes walk from it.

Whether or no, Bluebeard became a frequent visitor at Don Geronimo's, and it was not very long before Mercedita began to love the oily-tongued pirate, who knew so well how to mask his wickedness under a smooth exterior, aided by his handsome presence and affable manners. This, as a matter of course, was eminently satisfactory to Bluebeard, who shortly afterwards married her, and installed her as mistress of a house he had built near to the Castle. There he left her, after a short honeymoon, and supplying her plentifully with money he promised shortly to return.

Before leaving, he placed a locked Casket in her possession, along with the key, with the injunction to open it should he not come back again to her in the space of six months, but to beware how she did so till then.

All this, as in duty bound, Mercedita faithfully promised to observe, and for many days afterwards she shut herself up in her room from sheer grief at the loss of her pirate, just as the sweet Creole women of that island do to-day when their husbands leave them, for they are quite as soft-hearted and loving now as they were in the days of Bluebeard, aye, even as those were who lived in the days of Columbus. Not that Mercedita neglected at any time her household duties because of her love. There were the slaves to look after—and there were four of them—Simon Peter, Maria, Anita, and Jack, all of them of the true Mandingo type—black as sloes, and lazy as they always were, and are likely to be, while the tropical sun shines so brightly on those beautiful islands, and life is so easy to most of them. Then there was the stock to attend to, for Mercedita's kindness of heart extended to the whole of the animal kingdom; a dog, and a cat, and a goat from St. John, with a poor little motherless chicken she had picked up somewhere or the other, were her constant companions in-doors; while out-doors, a milch cow, a fine horse, and a litter of pigs completed the rest. And now that Bluebeard had gone she began to feel life lonely; her father rarely came to see her, and her female acquaintances were always too busy—maybe it was from a jealous feeling—for many of them had angled for the place that Mercedita now held in the pirate's affections.

So, amidst all the loneliness, what should Mercedita do but go up to the top of the Castle every day, and casting her eyes on the sea, look earnestly and searchingly all over the broad expanse of water for her husband's piratical schooner; this she did faithfully for over two months, when one evening, after remaining on the top of the Castle much later than usual, she went into her drawing-room where, on a table, she had placed the Casket that Bluebeard had left her; then the demon of curiosity possessed her and she took up the Casket.

"What is in it," she asked herself, as she turned it over and looked at it; "perhaps the secret of his life, the one thing that he keeps hidden away from me." Here she inserted the key. Then she began to tremble all over, partly from the strong desires which came over her, and the longing she felt to know the great secret she supposed it contained; then she gave the key a half-turn around, and from fear turned it back again, until, curiosity overmastering prudence, she gave it a complete turn and the Casket flew open, revealing nothing more than a bundle of letters tied up with a ribbon.

CHAPTER II.

WHEN the Casket flew open, Mercedita uttered a faint little cry; but when she saw the small package, with just a faint odour of perfume escaping from them, a feeling of jealousy came over her, which changed into that of rage and despair when she untied it, and saw that it contained seven different letters, each addressed to her husband in the hand of seven different ladies of her own social standing, and whom she had always looked upon rather as bosom friends than acquaintances.

How she found courage to read them I know not; but after conquering her scruples at thus playing the spy upon her husband's actions, she managed, amidst many sobs and feminine screeches, to get through them, gaining thereby an amount of information she did not formerly possess, and laying the foundation of a tragedy to which there had been nothing to compare in the annals of the island—not that she would have cared much if these letters had been merely the outpouring of affection from lovelorn women, admirers of Bluebeard. She, who loved him so much, always wondered why those who also loved him had not been as successful as herself in obtaining him; but these letters revealed such a depth of deceit on the part of her husband, and such a determination on the part of each of these women to take him from her, that, blind with rage and fury, she determined to be revenged on the whole lot of them—in other words, to make an example of them for the benefit of society.

At first she thought of making the letters public, but, on second thoughts, she came to the conclusion that everyone would merely laugh at her for doing so. Dismissing the idea, she went into a room where her husband had hung up against the wall a few old rapiers from Toledo, a sword and a dagger from Damascus.

This last she took down from the wall, and passed her finger along the keen edge of the blade with a feeling of grim satisfaction. Whether this was because she thought of killing her seven rivals, or her husband, or herself, I am not so certain, for, after a few moments' reflection, she put it back in its place on the wall again. Then she thought of all that Bluebeard would say when he came back to her—his rage at her fatal curiosity, her disobedience to his express commands so soon after he had left her; then she got frightened, and then, woman-like, she sat down on an ottoman and had a good cry.

A few moments spent thus and she got up again, returning to the drawing-room with the intention of replacing the letters in the Casket. This was not an easy task, for though she managed to tie up the letters in nearly the same form as they were before, she found she could not replace them in the Casket, which, by some peculiar arrangement of its mechanism, had become so distorted in shape, that it could neither be shut nor returned to its former appearance. Now whether it was that the contact of the letters, or this untoward behaviour on the part of the Casket, once again excited her anger, is difficult to say, but half an hour afterwards she found herself closeted with Mimmy Lafourche, the notorious Obeah woman from Martinique, who was driving quite a roaring trade with the credulous, of which there were many at that time, in St. Thomas. From this ugly old hag's hut she shortly after emerged with a small bottle of an infernal concoction which, the Obeah woman assured her, given to her friends, would entirely cure them of their passion for Bluebeard, and if given to him would make him her slave till death came to part them. As this was all the poor soul cared for to satisfy her peace of mind, is it to be wondered at that she invited her seven lady friends to take tea with her the following afternoon, which was Sunday?

A more lovely coterie of women never met in the island of St. Thomas, and Mercedita, who presided dressed in the purest white, looked more like an angel of innocence than the revengeful woman about to administer, to her unsuspecting guests, a native plant the real properties of which were unknown to her.

It is not told how she gave it to them, but it is quite sure that, shortly after partaking of a cup of tea, they all declared themselves dreadfully sleepy, and expressed an earnest desire to depart. As there were no cabs in those days these ladies were obliged to walk, and scarcely had they got to their homes, when they, each of them, went to bed and expired forthwith.

As it is natural to imagine, a great outcry went up against Mercedita at this untoward accident; seven husbands deprived of their wives, a host of children deprived of their mothers, and ever so many more deprived of seven staunch and dearly beloved friends.

Next morning the news reached Mercedita, who, half stupefied with grief at such a frightful calamity, was for giving herself up immediately to the strict arm of the law, to escape, if possible, the rage of the mob which would be surely excited against her upon hearing the whole truth of the story. So she sent for the Policemaster, and after frankly acknowledging to this official the sum total of her offence, she found herself about a half an hour afterwards an inmate of the place which, in those days, did duty as a prison for the more depraved of the townsfolk.

CHAPTER III.

CONSTERNATION reigned in the little town of Charlotte Amalia. Many an old burgher shook his head when he heard the story, magnified, of course, by being passed on from one to the other.

"All this comes from taking up with a pirate," said one.

"I always said she would never come to any good," said another.

And so on to the end of the chapter, each masculine or feminine fling being cast at Bluebeard or Mercedita—as the speaker was masculine or feminine—a noticeable fact being, that the men sympathized with Mercedita, and the women put in a saving clause for Bluebeard.

But the all-absorbing topic was, what would be done with her? The police investigation, then, was quite as strict as it is now, with this difference, that the thumbscrew and divers other little instruments of torture were employed when an offender refused to acknowledge his misdeeds. Of course, these were unnecessary with Mercedita, who, having made a clean breast of the matter, was duly held for trial, at the Town Court, on no less a charge than the doing to death of seven of her townswomen by sundry arts and practices called Obeah. The old sorceress had fled, whether put on her guard by one of her familiars or scenting danger as soon as Mercedita was arrested, is a question; but as I have before observed, the one thing which now occupied everyone's mind, was what would be done with her. And as the true story of what she had done had, somehow or the other, leaked out from the sacred precincts of the Court House, there seemed to be scarcely a doubt in the minds of the most charitably disposed, that she would be burnt as a witch, in spite of her youth and beauty, and the fact that she was the wife of so important a man as Bluebeard—for even such characters were considered so in those days, through their relations with the merchants, whom, it is said, often shared with them the proceeds of their plunder.

"What a lesson!" exclaimed an ancient spinster to a couple of friends—she had sinned in every way herself, until no longer capable of sinning, and now felt herself fit, as many another after a like experience, to pass judgment on such a poor unfortunate creature; "of course she will be burnt as a witch, eh! who would have thought it, so mild looking; but it is always the way with your mild looking hussies; they are generally the worst you know. What a disgrace to her family!" Now the truth is, Mercedita had no family—her mother died when she was a baby—only her father remained; and he, poor man, had been so thunderstruck at the news of his daughter's arrest, that he was almost bereft of his senses, and when after a long interview with her, which was kindly permitted him, and he heard the story of the Casket, he bitterly cursed the fatal curiosity which had induced Mercedita to open it, and Bluebeard himself, whom he half suspected as having devised this as a way for getting rid of his daughter, knowing full well that no woman could possibly resist the temptation of opening a Casket left with her under such conditions—as having the key to open it in her possession.

But the poor old man could do nothing but weep and bewail the hard lot which would condemn his child to a felon's fate, and bring down his grey hairs with sorrow to the grave. It was very affecting to see such grief on both sides, and even the hard-hearted jaolor who had, perforce, to be a witness of the sad interview, turned away his head and wiped away a tear, the only one he had shed for many a long day.

But there was no help for it, and it was not very long before Mercedita was brought up for trial and condemned to be burnt as a witch for having practiced sorcery. Of course, she was defended by the ablest lawyer who lived there; but vain was his plea. Had she only by some mischance, in some other fashion, without intention, done to death half the population, there might have been some excuse for her; but to have consulted an old Obeah woman—a thing which nearly everyone in the island had done—was not to be tolerated, especially, as she had confessed such iniquity. So nothing remained but for the judge to pass sentence of death, which was as follows:—That she be conducted to the sands of the sea, near to a place which is known as the King's wharf, and there, with a pile of faggots around her, she was to be burnt to death as an example to those, who, like her, dared to dabble in witchcraft. The sentence being approved of she was led away half fainting to prison, and not long after preparations were made for her execution.

CHAPTER IV.

Now, what was Bluebeard doing all this time that his wife was in such imminent peril? History nor the oldest inhabitant sayeth not; rumour credited him with having sunk and destroyed half-a-dozen merchant ships, laden with cargo and treasure; it also said that he would not come back again. Nevertheless, he was on his return to St. Thomas, where, by a singular coincidence, he turned up on the morning which was to see poor Mercedita burnt to death at the stake as a witch.

Little dreamt he that such a fate was in store for her as his gallant craft sailed into the fine harbour of St. Thomas. If he had been a general lover before he saw Mereedita, it must be said, to do him justice, that he loved her far more than anyone else, and as he cast his eyes upon the heights where he fondly supposed his beloved was looking out for him, his heart thrilled with delight at the thought of once more embracing her. But she, poor little woman, had made her peace with this world, had said adieu to her father and the few friends who had remained faithful to her to the last—she had even shaken hands with Simon Peter, Maria, Anita, and Jack—and could she have had one kiss, only one, from her own darling Bluebeard, she would willingly have gone to her death, so miserable had she been, so tried by the events of the past few days.

Was it by intuition or that subtle magnetism which betrays the proximity of a loved one, that she felt that Bluebeard was not far away from her? We confess our ignorance; but when the last of her visitors had gone, she moved a high stool close to the grating of the window which looked on to the harbour, and mounting it, it was not so long before she saw swiftly coming in what appeared to her to be her husband's vessel. Oh! how her heart beat when she caught sight of it, those beautiful lines, that sharp prow and, lastly, if her eyes did not deceive her, that gallant form standing on the poop giving orders.

"Thank God, I have seen him!" she exclaimed, as the vessel disappeared from the point of view from which she was gazing. "I have seen the man I love best on earth, I am now ready to die."

She never remembered, so great was her joy, that it was her husband's perfidy, and his leaving her with the Casket, that had caused her present misfortunes—such is the love of woman, her forgiving nature, her matchless constancy!

She had seen him; it was enough. More she did not dare to hope for. She was to die that afternoon; and though she could not doubt but what her husband would use every endeavour to see her, or to gain a last interview with her, she did not feel so sure that he would be successful—the authorities were strict to severity, and witchcraft was more severely punished than any other crime; so she sat down on the edge of the little pallet, which for so many days had been her couch, and let the tears course down her cheeks as they listed, only wishing that the whole thing was over and she at rest, where neither jealousy nor curiosity would any more torment her.

And here we will leave her for a little while, and take a look at Bluebeard who, impatient to reach his home again, had jumped into a cutter which lay alongside his schooner, and was being pulled, as fast as four oars could carry him along, towards the Castle.

A few minutes sufficed to bring him to the little landing-place fronting the pathway which led up to it, and a few minutes to the threshold of his home, where with almost a lover's impatience, he thought his wife would surely meet him.

But only the grief-stricken face of Anita encountered his as he stepped into the house—Jake, Simon Peter, and Maria had all gone in town to see the last of their dear mistress.

"Where's my wife?" inquired Bluebeard, a cold chill running through him at the thought that she was dead.

"Ay me massa, oh Gawd!' and here the girl burst into a flood of tears, sinking down on the ground as she did so, rocking herself backwards and forward in a wild lament.

"Speak woman, speak, where's my wife?" roared Bluebeard —now thoroughly anxious.

"Dey rest um."

"Rest um; what the devil do you mean?"

"She in prison sah, and dey go fo' burn her, dis afternoon, for one Obeah woman sah."

"Obeah woman, my wife an Obeah woman!" and Bluebeard almost laughed at the idea of his gentle Mercedita practising such arts as these. Then his eyes fell upon the Casket, which on taking up he found empty, and a dull suspicion crossed his mind that here was the cause of whatsoever trouble had befallen her; so, questioning the servant further, he gradually elicited from her as much as she knew of the story.

When she had done this, amidst many sobs and lamentations, he saw that not a moment was to be lost if he was to save Mercedita; so, hastily retracing his steps, he got into his boat again, and was pulled back to the schooner. Ten minutes after his arrival 50 of his men were armed to the teeth, and every boat the little vessel possessed—and she had a few more than the regulation number—was got ready for them.

Then Bluebeard went ashore, first arranging with his lieutenant to send after him 25 sailors as quickly as possible and to be ready to reinforce him with the rest if necessary. When Bluebeard reached the town, he went at once to His Excellency the Governor; but that high functionary would not see him. He then went to the judge; but he, acting in concert, perhaps, would not see him either. Nothing daunted, Bluebeard went to the Policemaster, but that high official was busy with the prisoner. This exasperated Blueboard, so he got someone to show him the place of execution. This being near the sea-shore, he dispatched a messenger to his lieutenant bidding him to send the men, and to be ready to sail out of the harbour at a moment's notice.

Shortly after they began to arrive, a few at a time, and mingling with the crowd, gradually got close to the pile of faggots near which stood the executioner.

Bluebeard had also placed himself not far away. Many of the crowd who knew him wondered how he could have had the bad taste to be present at his own wife's execution; but he heeded them not, only tightening the belt to which his hanger was attached, and feeling that his pistols were securely fastened beneath the jacket he had put on for the occasion.

Then the Fort bell began to toll in slow and solemn tones; a dozen soldiers with muskets marched upon the ground; by-and-by a procession, consisting of the judge, policemaster, and the officers of the law, made its appearance, bringing in their midst the prisoner, who, clad in a gown of white, a lighted taper in her hand, and her hair falling dishevelled all around her, presented a sorry spectacle to every one who looked at her. Bluebeard bit his nether lip till the blood came again when he saw the woman whom he best loved on earth in such a plight, and looked around, instinctively, at his crew, who, having got nearer to the pile of faggots, only awaited the word of command to come to her rescue.

Still the bell tolled on, its lugubrious sound helping to make the scene more doleful. Mercedita now, for the first time, saw her husband, and a thrill of joy ran through her frame at the sight of him; she had no fear of death then, its bitterness was past; he should see that she could die as bravely as the best of them. And now the old judge, putting on his spectacles, began to read out aloud how Mercedita, having murdered seven of her fellow-townswomen by sundry and divers arts magical, had been condemned to die by fire, as would be anyone who consulted wizards, witches, or such like enchanters.

This being done, Mercedita was brought before the executioner, who, without further ado, was about to tie her lily-white hands, when a blow from a handspike from one of Bluebeard's men knocked him senseless on the pile of faggots.

At the same time, Bluebeard's arm closed around the waist of Mercedita, and his men, gathering around him and his wife, began steadily to fight their way towards the sea, attacked at first by the soldiers, who, seeing the determined attitude of these daring sea-devils, soon desisted, finding themselves too few in numbers to cope with them; only the howling multitude pursued them to the water's edge, where, as soon as Bluebeard and Mercedita were safely embarked, and on their way to the schooner, many of them bit the dust at the hands of the infuriated pirates, who also had been sorely hit with the stones that they had flung at them. Not till they, too, were in their boats did the luckless crowd cease to get fired at, for, once roused, the pirates had no mercy. It was not long, however, before Mercedita and her husband, and the rest of his lawless associates, were on board, the lieutenant hoisting sail as soon as they were safe; but they were not to get out without an attempt on the part of the authorities to stop them, for just as the schooner was nearing the battery which, in those days, defended the entrance to the harbour, there was a perfect storm of round shot directed at the vessel.

At this Bluebeard's brow grew black as night, and, as one of them passed quite near to him, he shouted:—

"Show your teeth, my hearties"; and he ran up the black flag with his own hands, let fly a broadside at both batteries, and, with his long gun, dismantled a couple of cannon and killed half-a-dozen men who stood near to them.

"Give them another," he exclaimed as, under cover of the smoke, he forged ahead, with only a couple of rents in his canvas; this done, and the wind being favourable, they passed the point rapidly, and it was not very long before Bluebeard's schooner was hull-down on the horizon.

Here the legend ends so far. What became of Bluebeard and his wife, after he had rescued her, is not told. Report said that he took her to the Havana, where she afterwards died of a broken heart, the attractions of the Cuban ladies proving too much for him, in spite of the love he professed for her, and her jealousy preventing her from tolerating his flirtations with that Spartan-like equanimity which distinguishes some women. Another report said that she died peacefully in his arms at Tortuga, and he, broken-hearted at her death, went on pursuing his piratical courses until cut short by a British cruiser, which, after a desperate engagement, took him and the remnant of his crew to Jamaica, where they were hanged as pirates, as a warning to others.

Which of these reports is the true one I am not certain—the reader is welcome to believe either of them, just as he is the facts of the story I have written—whichever way it may be, I shall be pleased; but still more so, if I have enabled him to wile away a pleasant half-hour in its perusal.

"A REMARKABLE COINCIDENCE."

A STORY OF

BLUEBEARD'S CASTLE, ST. THOMAS, DANISH WEST INDIES.

CHAPTER I.

Mr. THEOPHILUS WIGGES was a shining light in Chicago.

This was in the year of the World's Columbian Exposition, that vast collection of buildings, that harmony in white, that reunion of all nationalities, which has done more to make the Windy City famous, than all the pork, beef, or mutton, that has ever been shipped out of it.

How Mr. Wigges came to occupy the important position that he held at the time that our story commences, might be told in a few words. It is the history of the greater part of America's millionaires. From the humblest beginnings to affluence. Battling at all times with overwhelming difficulties, triumphing always by sheer energy, pluck, and perseverance. Let no one suppose that those who now count their millions, where they once counted pence, have acquired them by sitting down with their hands folded. Read their histories, and see upon what small beginnings the Vanderbilts, Astors, and Rockefellers, founded their fortunes. Thus it was with Mr. Wigges. In the early days of Chicago, when its sidewalks were of wood, and the highest building was a three-storey dwelling, he sold "pop corn" on one of the streets leading into what is now known as Wabash Avenue; it is yet in the memory of many, what a trade he did in that delicious comestible, especially on the cold winter nights, when a handful of it, " smoking hot," was a good thing to keep the cold out.

Mr. Wigges was a young man then, full of what the Americans call "go," and there was no limit to his ambition—

as there were no limits to the "possibilities" of the Great West in those days.

Of course, such a character could not remain always a vendor of "pop corn," so, very soon, Mr. Wigges became the purchaser of an interest in a "Candy Factory," and not long after the sole proprietor thereof—for he was of a saving disposition and inventive withal; so much so, that with improved machinery and an ingenious method of advertising, he drove every competitor from the field.

For many years he worked at the business, early and late, perfecting it, and enlarging its sphere of operations to such an extent, that "Wigges' Candy" became a household word all over America.

At the same time he invested his profits in real estate, and its value increasing with the growth of the city, he rose higher and higher in the estimation of his fellow-citizens, and it was not very long before he became a partaker with them of the many good things which always offer themselves in such prosperous communities. And now finding life somewhat lonesome, he married, adding the "e" to his name, which makes it Wigges, becoming thereby the social equal of Mr. Figges, his father-in-law, the great pork butcher of Chicago.

Of course, his wife brought him money, all of which he cheerfully accepted, just as he had done everything else that Dame Fortune had hitherto showered upon him.

In the meanwhile Chicago had also prospered, and real estate advancing in value, some people turned a loving eye towards Mr. Wigges' investments, with the result that by-and-by he got an enormous sum for the lot where the Court House stands to-day. All this was very much approved of by his friends, who, as is usual in such cases, as soon as the tide of prosperity set in so strongly that no one could help seeing it, did their best to help him up a little further on the ladder of fortune—but not even these successful investments could turn him from his legitimate business; he already supplied nearly every western city with gum drops, and every lozenge conceivable that was ever made out of glucose or sugar—and not a young woman in Chicago commenced the day without masticating a few of them.

But it was not until he conceived the idea of combining pepsin with chewing gum—and decorated the whole city with gigantic posters setting forth its claims—that he achieved the crowning glory of his life, and became the shining light that we have stated at the beginning of this chapter.

As was natural in a place like Chicago, where minutes are golden, few business men at meal times ever stopped to chew their food rationally, and a chop or steak sometimes disappeared from their plates before they realized that it had been set before them; the consequence was, that dyspeptics were plentiful. To such as these, "Wigges' Chewing Gum" appealed strongly—it was so handy. Enough for a day's consumption could be carried in one's vest pocket, and as every second individual chewed it from morning until night, it was not long before Mr. Wigges was counted among the many millionaires of America. It was a bright idea, with the merit of giving satisfaction to those who used it, for once let the habit of chewing get the best of you, whether of tobacco, the end of your pencil, gum, or brown paper, it is very hard to leave off, and if ever a man deserved well of his fellow-creatures it was Wigges, who combined with innocent gum the virtues of pepsin for the benefit of dyspeptics. "There is nothing like it in the world," he would say enthusiastically to his friends. "It has made me rich, my home a happy one, and my workpeople contented. I have some specially prepared for Mrs. Wigges, whose curtain lectures I cut short by asking her to try it. As she cannot chew and scold at the same time, the result is peace, heavenly peace, which every one of you can attain by following my example." Not that Mrs. Wigges was a scold—far from it; she was really a good-tempered little woman, and perfectly worshipped her husband, with whom she had led a very happy life for nearly 20 years, devoting herself to his comfort and to the education of their only daughter Angelina, a charming young girl, who combined with beauty, vivacity, and intelligence, every feminine virtue.

Mr. Wigges doted on both of them; all that love and wealth could do, he bestowed upon them; their home was a sumptuous one—one of those palaces of Michigan Avenue which are the cynosure of all eyes and the wonder of the traveller. Mr. Wigges had but one trouble, and that was to keep away intruding fortune-hunters. There was a time when he had wished for a son, but now that woman was taking her proper place in the sphere of this world's usefulness, especially in Chicago, he did not mind it so much. With the hope of a good son-in-law, he lived perfectly content; and, having lately become a collector of coins—he had one of the finest collections in the world, got together at a vast expense—it might be said, that with this hobby indulged in to its fullest extent, with such an amiable wife, and such a charming daughter, Mr. Theophilus Wigges was not only a shining light, but the happiest man in the great city of Chicago.

CHAPTER II.

BUT as perfect happiness can scarcely be said to exist in this world, so was that of Mr. Wigges marred by the fact that if his collection of coins was the most perfect in Chicago, it yet lacked one coin to make it the most perfect in existence. There had never been more than two made, and that was somewhere in the first century; he had one of them, the other was—Heaven knows where. All that the most experienced numismatists could say about it was, that it was known to be in existence about two hundred years back, and that the man who could place that coin beside the one in Mr. Wigges' collection would be a made man for life, if he desired to part with it for a consideration, for it was an open secret that Mr. Wigges had offered a fabulous sum to anyone who would make him the fortunate possessor of it. Many an imitation had been offered him by unprincipled sharpers, who thought of trading upon his ignorance; but just as shrewd as Mr. Wigges was in the matter of trade in chewing gum or candy, he was equally so in numismatics, and many a kindred branch of science, which does not usually belong to the laity.

For let no one imagine that the prosperous American does not seek to improve his mind with his financial position. The term "shoddy" is wrongly applied to the American who has been the architect of his own fortune.

This brings us to the opening of the World's Columbian Exposition. As a matter of course, a man of Mr. Wigges' position and influence could not be left out in the bestowal of the "sugar plums" of office, which, somehow or the other, always accompanies such enterprises.

Mr. Wigges had modestly declined the post of Director-General of the Exposition in favour of the man " whose abilities to fill it," he said at a banquet not very long afterwards, " were so transcendently superior to his own, that he felt that he was doing Chicago a greater service by refusing, than if he accepted it."

So he was constituted an Honorary Director, which, as it did not involve much more than being present at the different " functions " in connection with the World's Fair, suited him admirably. It was in this character I first had the pleasure of meeting him, when, as Commissioner for the island of St. Thomas, Danish West Indies, to the World's Columbian Exposition, we placed on exhibition a model of that island in the Transportation Building, and so interested him in its attractive scenery and people, and the legends of its famous Towers, named after Bluebeard and Blackbeard, that he made up his mind to visit it as soon as the Exposition was over.

To be invited to Mr. Wigges' receptions was to be in the " swim " of Chicago society ; here, the " magnates of pork " and the " hustlers of wheat " and the " cornerers " of every known eatable out of which a dollar might be made by speculators met together ; here, their lovely wives and daughters were the admired of all observers, and these were many, of the best talent and birth, gathered from the four corners of the earth—the Englishman, the Frenchman, the Russian, and the Turk—there was scarcely a nationality unrepresented ; and the sweet women waltzed, chatted and laughed, flashing their bright eyes on everyone of them, and charming all of them with those sallies of brilliant wit and repartee which have made the American women famous throughout the civilized world. A distinguished gathering, presided over by a distinguished man, one who did honour to everything he put his hand to ; one who, by doing his best on all occasions, had drawn the best around him, and got the best out of a life which some are inclined to say is scarcely worth living ; but these are the lazy, discontented ones, and of such was not my honoured friend Theophilus Wigges.

It was at one of these receptions that I met my fellow-townsman, Mr. Algernon Divi-Divi, who had just come into his father's estates in St. Croix, the sister island of St. Thomas, in the Danish West Indies. I was very glad to meet him ; and, as he was one of the few from these islands at that time in Chicago, it did me good to see the face of an old acquaintance.

He had been but a few weeks in America, he said, and had come recommended to Mr. Wigges, who had received him with unbounded hospitality. Of Miss Wigges he spoke somewhat reservedly; but, from the looks of admiration that he cast upon her as she passed us leaning on the arm of the Turkish Commissioner, I could see that he was deeply smitten, and that more might come out of this visit of my young West Indian friend than Mr. Wigges expected. And here the reader might ask, " What right have you to tell tales out of school, and for which, having occurred so recently, you might possibly be called to account?" All I can plead is, that I have the permission of those most intimately concerned. If I have not, let them come forward and say so. This history of Mr. Theophilus Wigges, in connection with Bluebeard's Castle, is quite as true as any other legend which has been told of that edifice or island.

To make a long story short, Mr. Algernon Divi-Divi became a constant visitor at Mr. Wigges', was the devoted attendant of his daughter, won the favour of both parents, and before long the society papers had published the news of their engagement. Had these confined themselves to this it would not have mattered so much; but where they got their stories from, about Algernon Divi-Divi, I know not. One of the leading journals spoke of him as descended from an old West Indian family, the Cassadas, that his great grandfather had taken his name from a tree called "divi-divi," which grew in great profusion on his estate, and which had laid the foundation of his fortune. With a lack of geographical knowledge, peculiarly western, the editor had confounded St. Croix with St. Thomas, and planted Bluebeard's and Blackbeard's Castles on Mr. Divi-Divi's estate, thus constituting him their owner. The article in question darkly hinted at one of his ancestors having been Bluebeard himself, which so exasperated Mr. Algernon Divi-Divi, that he vowed he would take vengeance on the author wherever he might find him; but when he was informed that such stories were concocted to make the paper sell, and that his future father-in-law's career, quite as distorted, had been served up in one of the great dailies under the head of " Chicago's greatest benefactor, Wigges, the Chewing Gum Man," and was thought a huge joke, and was laughed at as a good advertisement, he became somewhat reconciled ; more especially as it was decided that next winter Mr. and Mrs. Wigges and their daughter would pay a visit to the island of St. Thomas, Danish West Indies.

CHAPTER III.

AND so it came about, that when the World's Columbian Exposition was a thing of the past, and Chicago was nearly snowed up, Mr. and Mrs. Wigges and daughter determined, now that the thermometer was at zero, to leave for the West Indies.

Messrs. Thomas Cook and Sons had by this time found out that these "Islands of the Sea" were beginning to have a special attraction for wealthy Americans; so, with their usual enterprise, promptly organised a party of tourists, and obligingly furnishing them with through tickets, pledged themselves, for a consideration, to see the visitors safely there and back again, barring accidents. To this very pleasant party Mr. and Mrs. Wigges and daughter belonged.

And now let us take a look at them approaching the harbour of St. Thomas, Danish West Indies, after five days' steaming from the city of New York.

Mr. Wigges had never been much of a traveller in foreign countries. He had taken a trip once to the Bahamas, and on another occasion had paid a visit to Florida; but as he stood on the deck of the "Orinoco," which then, about a mile from the port, was slowly nearing it, and gazed upon the scene before him, he felt that he had never looked upon anything so beautiful before in his life. Rising almost straight out of the water were heights, varying from 800 to 1500 feet, which, owing to rains having fallen plentifully a few days before, were covered with luxuriant vegetation in all shades of green—from the lightest to the darkest. In striking contrast to this mass of verdure, the town, with hundreds of red-roofed houses, rose to the summits of three hills, as a justly celebrated author once said of them, "looking for all the world like a box of toys shaken down its slopes." And it was not long before he made out Bluebeard's and Blackbeard's Towers—the first to the east of the town, and the latter to the north of it, facing the entrance, and overlooking the little red Fort below. Just then there was quite a number of ships in the harbour, at least half a dozen men-of-war of different nationalities; among them the stars and stripes floated from one of Uncle Sam's smart looking cruisers. Mr. Wigges made a note of this particularly; indeed, the sight of that dear old flag made his eyes grow dim for the moment, and I am not quite sure whether a tear did not fall on his note-book as he did so. Practical even when overcome by emotion, Mr. Wigges did not fail also to place on record his opinion as to the value of St. Thomas as a Naval and Coaling Station to that country of which he was so distinguished an ornament.

His wife and daughter were equally interested: they compared the balmy weather of the West Indies with the fearful cold they had left behind them; the happy looks of the dusky boatmen, which were now crowding about the vessel, with the half-frozen appearance of the longshoremen upon whom they had last looked when leaving New York; and novel and strange as it all appeared to them, yet they could not help agreeing that their voyage, thus far, had not been in vain.

I am certain Miss Wigges felt so; and when Mr. Algernon Divi-Divi stepped on board, after the "Orinoco" had been given pratique, she was the happiest young girl on the steamer that morning; and her dear old *pater*, Mr. Wigges, thought so too, as he witnessed their meeting, and, no doubt, felt correspondingly happy, for she was his only child, his darling, the apple of his eye.

And now let us follow them to one of the best boarding-houses in Charlotte Amalia, where they were to stop for a few weeks, prior to leaving for the island of St. Croix, the home of her intended. They preferred this quiet retreat to the bustle of the hotel, and, as the place was delightfully situated, and had a lovely garden adjoining, our young lovers pictured to themselves several days of happiness before them. I have said that Mr. Algernon Divi-Divi owned sugar estates in the island of St. Croix. In reality, he was one of the largest proprietors, was looked upon as a wealthy man—at least, for that island, where millionaires are only known by repute, or when, like Mr. Wigges, it is their good pleasure to visit it.

Now if there is a thing in this world that affords greater pleasure than being the owner of a sugar estate, it is that of not being one, especially when the weather is dry, prices are low, and the expenses running on—and run on they must, for a sugar estate cannot be brought so easily to a full stop, or turned into a coffee or a tobacco plantation all at once.

Unfortunately for Mr. Algernon Divi-Divi, he had inherited more than one sugar estate, which, while producing good crops and realizing fair values during his father's lifetime, were far from being profitable investments to him.

For many years America had been the best market for West Indian sugars, just as the West Indies are for American provisions, which have enjoyed all the privileges accorded to the most favoured nation, in the same way that West Indian sugars did certain privileges from America; but of late, what with the accession of a party of slippery politicians into power at Washington, and, in consequence, a Government from whom no nation could expect reciprocity, or any treaty to be binding, the outlook had become so gloomy for these islands, that nothing but bankruptcy stared them in the face. Of all this Mr. Wigges was perfectly ignorant. Like most of his well-to-do countrymen, he thought America the best country, its people the greatest on earth : he, too, had been a politician, but, whether from use or second nature, he looked upon their wiles as part of the great game of life in which all men ought to play. He did not, of course, endorse right down chicanery; but all was fair to him in matters political. It always seemed to him the correct thing to undo all the Democrats did when they were in power, just as, no doubt, the Democrats have felt it their bounden duty to do by the Republicans when they came out of office. That all this should have any far-reaching consequences outside America, or that American politics should be looked upon with mistrust and suspicion by every other nation never once occurred to him, as, very likely, it is the case with thousands of America's best men and citizens who have allowed their truly great country to become the prey of an unscrupulous oligarchy.

The fact was there nevertheless, and Mr. Wigges was soon brought to understand it when Algernon Divi-Divi, in a frank and open manner, laid his position before him. As may be imagined, this was a great shock to him. Mr. Wigges was not really an avaricious man. He would have cheerfully surrendered his daughter to the man she loved if he were not worth a dollar; but it jarred upon his sense of the fitness of things that his daughter should marry a ruined sugar planter.

It is true, his own wealth was amply sufficient to sustain his son-in-law through any possible commercial crisis; but he had been so happy when he saw his name coupled in the great dailies of Chicago with that of Algernon Divi-Divi, the Spreckels of St. Croix, the sugar of whose estates would go to swell his own importations, that he felt almost as miserable as Algernon himself when he told him of his reverses. He had planned more than one scheme in connection with his future son-in-law; had even contemplated bringing out a special West Indian Chewing Gum, in which the delicious aroma of the Bayberry and St. Croix muscovado would be so skilfully blended as to delight the American public, if not the civilized world, and now all these bright dreams would be dashed to the ground.

"All through those accursed Democrats," he muttered, as he walked up and down the piazza, after a somewhat unsatisfactory interview with Algernon Divi-Divi.

Then he thought of his daughter. What would she think of it? He had anticipated so much pleasure from this trip, and now how was it to end? He almost wished Algernon had kept him in the dark, at least, for the present. In this frame of mind he kept on walking about, his only solace being a piece of chewing gum, and if it had not been for a young man presenting himself at that moment, with a rare old Danish five-stiver piece for his inspection, which at once absorbed his attention, there is no knowing how I should have got to the end of this chapter.

CHAPTER IV.

THE only one who did not seem very much put out by the turn things had taken was Miss Wigges. Accustomed all her life to live in luxury, to have all she wanted, and to consider herself the heiress to her father's many millions, she looked upon what had happened to her lover, when he told her of his reverses, as a mere bagatelle, which her father would remedy in "no time," as she tersely expressed it.

Imagine her surprise, when her father, in a somewhat matter-of-fact way, informed her of his intention of shortly leaving St. Thomas for a tour of inspection of the rest of the West Indies, and that, for the present at least, she must look upon her engagement with Mr. Divi-Divi—he no longer called him Algernon—at an end.

But she did not cry, not a bit of it, nor did she speak disrespectfully; she simply asked to be fully informed of her father's reasons, to which, when given her, she replied, with fine scorn and a flush of indignation spreading over her fair features:

"So, it is a question of money, after all! Now, my dear father, I thought you admired principle beyond anything; but —and forgive me for saying so—you are acting as badly now as those Democrats have been doing to these islands. You will remember there was no talk of his wealth in Chicago; it was merely a question whether he loved me, and I loved him. I 'banked' on Algernon's love, he 'banked' on mine, just as the West Indies 'banked' on America keeping its pledges. Now, you find it suits you to back out, and you become just as—well, I do not wish to speak disrespectfully to you, I love you too much, but I must say it in one way—just like those Democrats; but there is one thing you have not counted on, I do not intend to back out, come what will. And, now, allow me to wish you a very good morning"; and before Mr. Wigges could recover from his astonishment—she had never spoken to him like that before—she had kissed him, and run out of the room, going straight to her mother.

But there her spirit failed her, and five minutes afterwards she was sobbing out her disappointment and sorrow in the arms of that good lady, who, much as she loved her husband, was deeply pained at his sudden determination, not understanding herself how Algernon Divi-Divi's misfortunes, in no way the result of his own imprudence, could have so influenced him with regard to their daughter, whom she knew he loved beyond anything—even his money—aye, even herself whom he had loved for so many years so faithfully and so well.

And now night stole over all these troubled minds—a lovely tropical night—in which everything under the light of the moon shows so brightly, in which the palm trees softly rustle their leaves, the flowering cacti and jessamine give out their perfume, and everything is so peaceful and still. Mr. Wigges had long ago sunk to rest; Mrs. Wigges slumbered on at his side. Miss Wigges had cried herself to sleep in the adjoining apartment; only Algernon Divi-Divi remained awake, tossing restlessly on his bed, wishing for daylight as he thought over the cruel fate which so soon was to separate him from his sweetheart. By-and-bye he, too, fell asleep: not even such sorrow as his was proof against Nature's balmy restorer, man's best friend in all his troubles.

How long he slept he could not tell, but somewhere about midnight he awoke and, to his astonishment, sitting by his bedside was the quaintest figure he ever saw in his life. Dressed in a blue coat with gilt buttons, knee-breeches, and buckles to his shoes, with a cocked hat on his head, lace ruffles to his sleeves, with a pair of pistols stuck in his belt, and a hanger by his side, he sat calmly surveying our hero as if it were the most natural thing in the world for him to do.

"Don't be alarmed," he said, taking a pinch of snuff from a box all covered with diamonds, and which glittered brightly in the moonbeams which played through the jalousies of the room. "I'm Bluebeard, or his ghost if you like, for I daresay that it seems impossible to you for such a resuscitation to take place after so many years have passed; at any rate I'm your friend, as, in the old days, I was always of every one in these islands when in trouble or difficulties. I daresay you have heard of me before, and of my good friend Blackbeard who used to own the other place on the hill yonder."

Here our hero thought he was telling fibs, but did not dare to say so.

"Don't doubt me!" exclaimed Bluebeard ferociously. "For all they have said and done, they have never been able to take away our names from the two old Towers, and as long as they last they will be called after us. But I have said I am your friend, and so I am sure you will eventually find out if you follow my advice, which is this. You have heard, of course, that we once buried a lot of treasure up there. Well, so we did, and in a great many other places, all of which have been pretty nearly ransacked by now. Anyhow, what I want you to do, is to go up to my Tower and look carefully round the old building, where, in a crevice to the east, which no one has ever remarked before, and no one will ever again after you, you will find something which, if rightly used, will bring Mr. Wigges to his senses and secure you the hand of his daughter."

"But the Tower is not my property, and if I should find anything there it will not belong to me," replied Algernon.

"Never you mind, do as I tell you; the Tower belongs to me, and so does everything you may find in it; besides, what you will find is given to you by me. No one else, not even the present owner, can give it to you. Anyway, do as you are told, if you wish to be happy. Farewell"; and in a flash he was gone, leaving our hero fast asleep again.

Of course, when Algernon awoke he felt inclined to laugh at his dream, but it was one which continued to haunt him from the time that he got out of bed; so much so, that impelled by a power that he could not withstand, he took the road to the Tower.

He found no difficulty in getting there, and no one to interfere with his inspection of it. The owner had gone with his family on a trip to St. Lucia, and the only watchman had gone into town on his own business.

Twice he walked round the Tower, and more than once looked up at its frowning walls as he did so, but on his third round sure enough there was a chink in the wall lying invitingly open. He had not noticed it before, in fact, he could have sworn that no such chink existed, but there it was, and lying snugly ensconced at the bottom of it was a package; this he carefully pulled out and opened, discovering an old coin of beautiful design.

He was no numismatist or he might have been able to appreciate its freshness and beauty; as it was, he only sighed from disappointment; for when he first took out the package he thought that, after all, his dream might come true, and perhaps a diamond of great value might be concealed in it, the remnant may-be of Bluebeard's treasures. Indeed, so great was his chagrin, that he felt almost inclined to throw it away, but remembering, after all, that it was a remarkable coincidence— no pun is intended—he descended the hill, and wended his way slowly homewards.

It was a lovely morning, and he might have felt the happiest man alive if it had not been for the ill-fortune which had overtaken him. Sitting down for a moment upon a little bench near at hand, he drew out the coin and looked at it.

"Singular, isn't it!" he said softly to himself. "It looks very old and quaint, looks as if it had seen some good times in its day. Money of the olden time, did you ever cause such misfortune to mankind as your prototype of to-day? Were you as much the golden calf then as you are now? What a lot you could say if you could speak! What——"

"Yes, Algernon dear," said a sweet voice behind him. "What a lot that old coin is going to do; you'll find out presently when we take it to my father. We may safely trust its past history with him, in face of the good it will bring to us." And here, Miss Wigges, who was also out for a morning walk, sat down beside her lover and looked at the coin.

"Why, it's the very one my father has been looking for for the last ten years. He has offered an enormous sum for it; has notified collectors all over the world his desire to obtain it at any price. Why, he won't hesitate to part with me for it."

"But my dear—you in exchange for such an old coin as this? A billion such would not suffice to buy you from me."

"Certainly not. If there were a billion of them—but this is the only one besides the one now in the possession of my father. And then you know, Algernon, you are not a numismatist, and therefore not supposed to know its value, but really, how did you come to find it?"

Then he told her of his dream about the pirate Bluebeard, and his scruples about appropriating it.

"Nonsense!" my dear Algernon, "didn't Bluebeard come himself to give it to you? Come, let's get home at once, and let papa see if it is really the right one or not."

And as her word was law just then with Algernon they did so, placing the coin in the hands of her father, to his unbounded astonishment and delight. In all his life he had not experienced such a surprise. He, certainly, never expected to complete his magnificent collection of coins in St. Thomas. It was marvellous!—and in the manner in which it had occurred. Why, it would fill six columns of the *Chicago Tribune*, and create such a sensation among the numismatists as would crown him with glory for the rest of his days. Consent to their marriage? Why, of course he would!

The truth of it is, that he had made up his mind to do so before they came in; his was a kindly nature, and the gentle reproaches of his wife had softened him considerably.

At that moment Mrs. Wigges entered the room, and when she heard the whole story, the tender-hearted creature broke down completely for joy.

"Bless the old Pirate," she said, as she affectionately kissed her husband, and threw her arms round his neck; whether she meant Mr. Wigges or Bluebeard has never been told, but I do know that they solemnly blessed the young couple, who were married and lived happily ever afterwards.

"BLACK IVORY."

CHAPTER I.

It is a moot question whether Mr. James Teach really did care to reside on the hill where Blackbeard's Tower had stood for over a century.

The Tower itself was out of repair; and when Mr. James Teach leased it, with the adjoining buildings, the upper floor was only accessible by means of a ladder from below, the first and second floors having crumbled away before the inroads of time and the wood-worm, which spares scarcely anything in the shape of woodwork in the West Indies.

The two small houses which, at that time, stood near to it, were in a little better condition; and when Mr. Teach had expended a few dollars in necessary repairs, they were quite habitable.

Yet it was a wonder to the busy town's folk, who passed their lives money grubbing at the foot of the hill and along the shore of the beautiful bay which makes St. Thomas the possessor of the finest harbour in the West Indies, why Mr. Teach had chosen to leave the spacious house he occupied on the Main Street for such uncomfortable quarters.

Various were the comments, and more than one hinted that it was only another of the mysterious ways of Mr. Teach that had made his life so unaccountable to the rest of the community. Others said, that perhaps he was going to dig for treasure; but as several persons had dug up half the place already, with the same object, the idea was scouted.

They were a busy people in those days. Anyone—a white man with the least ability—could make money; and they were, as a rule, so occupied, that they soon forgot the circumstance of Mr. Teach occupying the Tower; though some busybodies, who had nothing else to do, did not fail to notice that he mounted to the top of it every morning early, remaining there more than an hour scanning the horizon with his telescope.

Not that there was anything extraordinary in that, for he owned several vessels; among them, two or three rakish-looking schooners which traded between St. Thomas and the island of Porto Rico. And here again was another mystery; each of these schooners carried a long swivel-gun at the stern, for their protection against pirates, so Mr. Teach said; though his friends and the public asserted, between themselves as a matter of course, that these guns were for piratical purposes.

Now all this may have been very true; but so cautious were the dealings of Mr. Teach, that he never gave any one just cause to be certain that he had any connection with that kind of gentry; though it is a notorious fact, that more than one rich and prosperous trader in St. Thomas gave assistance to the pirates which infested West Indian waters; but Mr. Teach had never but once, during his residence of ten years on the island, given cause for the slightest suspicion, and then he had so promptly placed his books at the Government's disposal, and offered his house and office so readily for its inspection, that the officials apologized for even suspecting him.

But this did not satisfy those malicious persons who are never satisfied that a man can get along in the world without being a rogue or a rascal, so they even went so far as to insinuate that Mr. Teach had bribed them to overlook the most glaring facts against him; which horrible calumny, when it came to their ears, made them more blind than ever to anything that Mr. Teach did in the prosecution of his honourable calling.

Now what was the honourable calling that Mr. James Teach followed in the town of Charlotte Amalia?

Let us go back a little into Mr. James Teach's history.

Some years before this story opens he began life in Anegada. Who were his parents, where he was born, and in what condition of life, does not concern us at this moment; we only know him at that period of his existence as a stalwart young man, named John Block, living in a small cabin by the sea-shore, eking out a precarious livelihood by fishing. The island at that time was peopled by more whites than at present; in fact, only a few escaped slaves from the neighbouring islands helping the whites, who were to all intents as poor as themselves.

We might have said equally as ignorant, for amongst all of them John Block was the only one who could read, write, and cipher. How he came by these accomplishments was best known to himself; though rumour pointed to his having been taught by his mother, who claimed to be of respectable parentage, but why she ever came to such a barren place as Anegada was a matter of surprise to the islanders.

John Block was of a moody disposition, and cared but little for the companionship of his fellows. When not fishing he plaited fishpots, in the same manner as the "Cha Cha" does to-day; or he built boats, at which he was very skilful. For these he got a good price; and as his expenses were next to nothing, by-and-bye he became talked about as well-to-do in the world— the little world of Anegada—and more than one girl, of the few in the island, cast "sheep's eyes" at him; all of which was entirely lost upon John Block, who had not a particle of love in his composition for any other human being in this world than himself—a more selfish vagabond, probably, never existed.

How long John Block might have vegetated in this manner it is difficult to say; but one day the sky grew dark, great clouds gathered overhead, the sea rose in its might, the wind blew a hurricane, and every living soul on that island crept into his hut with fear and trembling in his heart that he might never live to see another morning. It was one of those fearful gales, for which the West Indies is famous, sweeping all before it, and carrying destruction to the homes of thousands.

For John Block such convulsions of Nature had no special terrors. He had no beliefs to worry him; no fears of hell; no hopes of a heaven; he believed in himself. His cabin was a strong one, made to withstand the greatest storm; and all that fearful night, after he had crept into it and fastened himself securely in, he slept as soundly as if the gentlest wind were lulling him to sleep.

And when morning brought Nature smilingly contemplating all the havoc and desolation she had made, in just such a mood came forth John Block to look how things had gone with his fellow islanders. Not that he loved them enough to help them; but, if his assistance were paid for, he would have been ready enough to give it.

But most of them lived at a distance, and in order to reach them he would have to pass along a considerable stretch of sea-shore. Selecting a stout stick from among several that stood in the corner of his cabin, he started, making his way with considerable difficulty, as a great deal of sea-wreck and *débris* had been washed up by the waves, which yet were angrily lashing the beach.

He had not gone far before he came across the body of a man.

It was not the first time, by any means, that he had seen a body cast up by the sea; but this was not an ordinary person. Ignorant as he was of what life really was outside of Anegada, he had read enough, in the few books he had managed to procure, of how people looked and lived in other countries. One thing was sure, this man was a very much superior person to any one he had ever seen before, dead or alive. He had a dim remembrance, when he was a child, of a visit to that island by the Governor of Tortola, and how he had shrunk close to his mother when that high and mighty personage looked at him; but here was some one whose appearance betokened a higher station than the Governor.

His first thought was to see if he was alive, and if so, to help him or to seek assistance to carry out this charitable impulse; his second, and that came more naturally to him, was to make sure he was dead, by hitting him over the head with his stick, and then to rob him.

A fine diamond ring, an elegant watch and seals, and, enclosed in a waterproof cover, a pocket-book heavily lined with English bank notes for £100 each, rewarded him for his pains.

Having secured these, and made sure that there was nothing more to appropriate, he returned back to his hut, and seating himself on a log, which served him for a stool, he began to think.

And the upshot of his thoughts was to leave Anegada as soon as possible, get to Tortola, and thence to St. Thomas; then the Emporium of the Antilles, where fortunes were made, where the scum of the West Indies met and hobnobbed, and where no one would ask him whence he got those £100 bank notes.

CHAPTER II.

WE shall pass over the years that James Teach, formerly known as John Block, took to become, first, a burgher, and then a man of consequence, in the island of St. Thomas.

He may be said to have started fairly in the world with the capital which he had acquired so infamously from the body that the sea had washed on shore at Anegada, and as there was plenty to do in the town of Charlotte Amalia for a man with money at his command, it was not long before he found out the right way to employ it. At that time St. Thomas was a rendezvous for almost every craft that sailed in West Indian waters—as many as 100 to 175 vessels might have been counted at once in its harbour. All the produce of the Spanish Main passed through it on its way to Europe. Vast cargoes of merchandise came out in return, which were sold to the countless purchasers that constantly visited it. It was also the headquarters for an enormous traffic in slaves, and though the Danish Government had declared it unlawful, it was not entirely suppressed when James Teach landed, and many men were said to have made large fortunes by shipping them to Porto Rico and the other islands.

It was a quick and easy way to wealth when properly managed, and James Teach was not slow to perceive that this was as good a way as any to invest his money, if he desired to reap a quick return for it.

Not but what there were many risks to encounter; first and foremost, the Government officials, who were very strict and attentive to their duties when a cargo of "black ivory," as a shipload of Africans was called in those days, was expected to be smuggled into port; but James Teach went systematically to work. Finding his capital too small to carry out his plans of importing them direct, he bought one of the fastest schooners afloat, and, engaging a picked crew from among the desperadoes who were such frequent visitors to St. Thomas he made himself her captain, and, after a year's cruising, he had realized enough to dispense with commanding her himself, and to purchase several other vessels, all engaged ostensibly in commerce with the islands.

His method possessed, at least, the merit of originality— a good slave was worth any day from 300 to 500 dollars in Porto Rico. To send to Africa for a cargo demanded special vessels, considerable outlay, and involved not only the risk of meeting British cruisers on the way, but the liability of loss by the death of half the cargo before reaching its destination.

All this James Teach avoided by the simple plan of waylaying nearly every slave vessel bound to the West Indies, murdering captain, officers, and crew, and appropriating every other living soul on board that could be called an African.

As he took care to scuttle the ship afterwards, on the specious plea that dead men tell no tales, there was nothing left to bear witness against him but his own crew, who, being accomplices and sharers in the spoil, were not likely to turn king's evidence against him.

His greatest difficulty, at first, was to stow them away before a favourable opportunity offered for shipping them to Porto Rico, without exciting the suspicion of the Danish authorities; but, after he had more than doubled his capital by a successful venture or two, he purchased one of the largest houses on the Main Street, and, with the aid of his ship carpenters, constructed, unknown to anyone else, a hiding-place, capable of concealing 100 slaves, between two of the loftiest rooms in the dwelling. So skilfully did they manage it, and its secret entrance, that for years, long after James Teach's death, no one suspected its existence; here, at midnight, when everything was quiet in the town and harbour, he would bring the unfortunate slaves, each one bound and gagged, and lay them, like trussed fowls, close to each other, until he was ready to ship them away.

As we have before remarked, in the introductory chapter, though strongly suspected, he was never found out; only those connected with his nefarious schemes knew of them, and they were too well paid and deeply mixed up in them to betray him; besides, men's consciences were very elastic then on the subject of "black ivory"—a coloured man was hardly credited with being a human, and as for his having any rights in particular, they were only laughed at; only the Government, so often accused of being the oppressor, seemed to have discovered that this traffic in flesh and blood was unlawful; and it must be said that its suspicions were strongly excited against Mr. James Teach.

In the meantime many merchants of St. Thomas, who were interested in the direct importation of "black ivory" from Africa, lost several valuable cargoes with their vessels; but as nothing ever was heard of either, they were, rightly or not, put down as lost at sea.

And now, having thrown a little light on the honourable calling which Mr. Teach pursued so much to his satisfaction, and that of his associates, we will pass to the only redeeming episode in his remarkable career, and which, being based on pure selfishness from the beginning, would be hardly worth mentioning, if it were not necessary to our story, as illustrating the manner in which the most secret crimes become known, and are punished in the end.

From the earliest days of the colony the women of the island had been noted for their beauty, especially the Creoles of two or three generations; but though Mr. James Teach, in virtue of his great wealth, and his having become a very important man in the community, had been thrown in contact with some of the handsomest, his heart, if he had any, remained untouched.

As we have once before observed, all the love he had was for himself; nothing else up to then had shared it; not even his dog could get a caress from him.

There was one girl, however, who had caught his fancy, but she was a mere child, not yet 13 years of age when he first saw her.

She lived with her aunt in a tumble-down cottage on the confines of the town, where they earned their living by ironing and starching fine things, and sewing for their neighbours. Now James Teach had noticed Eva Wilson more than once during his walks in the country; and strange enough to relate, conceived a violent passion for her, and had she been older would have sought her in marriage at once; but in view of the fact that she was so young, he interviewed her aunt, and proposed to her to send them away to Copenhagen, there to have her educated, and if she were willing, at the end of five years he would make her his wife.

Only one thing he insisted on, and that was strict secrecy. This the elder woman promised, and as she saw no reason to doubt the word of so reputable a man as James Teach, she, without even consulting her niece, accepted his offer, leaving for Denmark a few weeks after. This occurred about four years before our story opens, and may be said to be the only good action ever done by Mr. James Teach in the whole of his blood-stained career. How he was impelled to do it is an insolvable riddle, unless that Nemesis, which almost always follows crime, had selected this fair young girl as the means to effect his destruction.

CHAPTER III.

Now let us follow Eva Wilson and her aunt to Copenhagen, then, as now, one of the cleanest and best regulated cities in Europe.

Voyages to and from the Danish West Indies and the Mother Country, for so the colonists have ever loved to call Denmark, were much more serious affairs than they are at this time, very seldom being accomplished by the old merchant vessels of the Eighteenth Century under three months. They were stoutly built, and in many instances had elegant passenger accommodations. It was in one of these that they reached Denmark, after a pleasant voyage of one hundred days. They bore excellent letters to Mr. James Teach's agent, then the head of one of the most substantial firms in Copenhagen, and who, knowing him to be a man of great wealth in St. Thomas, extended a cordial welcome to them, and, for the time being, the hospitality of his home. This sudden transition from the drudgery they had formerly passed through was not without its effect on Eva's aunt, who, from a careworn, anxious-looking woman became almost young again in the atmosphere of kindness which surrounded her. As for Eva, the best masters were secured for her, and everything done to carry out the wishes of Mr. Teach, with regard to her education. And she responded nobly to their efforts to improve her. With a natural aptitude for the acquirement of knowledge she progressed rapidly, and as the years rolled over her head she developed not only in the matter of every accomplishment taught at that period, but actually excelled in others not generally considered as belonging to her sex.

She corresponded regularly with Mr. Teach, giving him, according to his wish, a minute account of her daily life, her progress in her studies, and her impressions of everything around her. She had learned by this time to consider him her best friend and benefactor, and even to look upon him with considerable affection for all that he had done for her.

Her aunt, who saw the end of the period of probation expiring, took pains to place Mr. Teach in the most favourable light before her, always taking care not to let her know the secret of her ultimate destiny, fearing to alarm her, and perhaps to engender hatred, where it was desirable she should feel nothing but love.

In the meanwhile, Eva's beauty had become the theme of admiration of everyone. Moving among the wealthiest and most fashionable people in Copenhagen, known as the adopted daughter of the richest man in the Danish West Indies, she had scores of admirers at her feet, and might, had she chosen, have married with the best of them. But charming as she was in her demeanour, gentle as she was in all her ways, and friendly as she was in disposition, not one of them could boast of ever having received a favour at her hands, nor one word of encouragement from her lips. All this was duly repeated by the aunt to Mr. James Teach, who, in a sort of madness which seemed to have possessed him as far as this young girl was concerned, thought that it was because of her love for him that she cared for no one else. And so this went on, steadily gaining possession of him every day, the passion of love consuming him finally to such an extent, that at times he would neglect his business merely for the sole pleasure of thinking of her.

And when at last the five years expired that he had set aside for the completion of her education, he could no longer contain himself, and at once wrote letters for their return by one of the first vessels leaving for the Danish West Indies, fully expecting to marry her upon her arrival.

And now a strange thing happened as this letter was crossing the ocean to its destination; a certain Danish nobleman addressed her, and, what is stranger still, succeeded in breaking down that barrier of icy reserve with which she had treated everyone else. Of winning presence, and endowed with rare mental gifts, His Excellency, Count Lauritz, would have been called a very handsome man if it had not been for a frightful scar just over the forehead, which he said he had received when shipwrecked and cast ashore at a place called Anegada, in the great hurricane which took place ten years before in the West Indies.

Whether it was the fact of his having escaped such peril so near to her own dear native land, or whether his stories of adventure, for he had travelled much, impressed her so that like another Desdemona, in listening to them, her love went out towards him, we know not: but it is very certain that by the time Mr. Teach's letter reached them, she had pledged her troth to him. This at first sight may appear extremely blameable on her part; but as Mr. James Teach had never breathed a word of love in any of his letters, and as the aunt had never mentioned his ultimate designs, in return for having launched them into good society and educated Eva, it seems most natural that things should turn out in this manner; indeed it could not be otherwise, for surely no one would have cared to see her married to such a wretch as Mr. Teach had proved himself to be on all occasions, excepting this.

Why the aunt did not inform her is the only thing to wonder at, but living in a fool's paradise all the time, she never thought of it; perhaps she did not care to spoil her niece's present happiness. She really loved her, and had no particular desire to see her wedded to Mr. James Teach. So when a scion of one of the noblest houses in Denmark presented himself, she never said a word, but actually joined their hands and congratulated them when he told her of their engagement. Then it was that Mr. Teach's letter stared them in the face.

This, however, was quietly got over by Eva; who, with true feminine intuition, having some misgivings as to his approval of her choice without consulting him, said that they would get married first and afterwards ask his blessing on the union. To this Count Lauritz cordially consented; and as he, just about that time, received a royal appointment as Commissioner to the Danish West Indies, for the purpose of investigating certain acts of piracy and slave-dealing which had occurred in Danish waters, it was decided that they should get married at once, and then leave Copenhagen in the first vessel bound for the West Indies.

CHAPTER IV.

THUS it is, that some three months afterwards we find them in the tropics, not far from their journey's end, and becalmed about fifty miles off the coast of Anegada.

A very slight breeze had sprung up during the last twenty-four hours, but scarcely sufficient to move the huge, lumbering vessel which had taken them thus far towards their destination.

The captain, an old and experienced mariner, looked anxiously aloft at his sails flapping idly against the masts, and more than once swept the horizon with his glass for the sign of any strange craft.

With a precaution born of experience, he had seen that the few muskets and cutlasses the ship possessed were in proper order, and the two carronades well cleaned and loaded with a full charge of grape. He kept a strict look out also, for he knew that many a fine ship had met her doom in these waters, at the hands of the blood-thirsty pirates that infested them. How he whistled for a good wind, a spanking breeze to send him bowling along at ten knots an hour into harbour, where, at any rate for awhile, his anxiety would be over. But that breeze would not come for the vessel he commanded; there was only just enough to fill the sails of one of Mr. James Teach's schooners, which had been on the look out for plunder for a fortnight. First, her topmasts showed above the horizon, then her mizen masts, and then her long black hull came creeping up to them, slowly but surely, just as the tiger crawls upon its prey.

Not even the dead calm which set in checked her progress, for the pirate captain got out his sweeps, and when within a mile of of them ran up the black flag, and fired his swivel gun at the rigging of the unlucky "Dagmar."

Down came some of the top gear with a crash, but doing no further damage than smashing a hen-coop.

"Oh, for a gun like that!" exclaimed the Danish captain, as another shot came crashing into his ship; "run up the Dannebrog, my lads, and let them see when they do come on board what a welcome we can give them. There will be no quarter for any of us if they take us, so we may as well fight it out with them."

By this time the deck was clear for action. The men were armed and the guns moved aft, so that they would be able to sweep the deck with grape-shot. The ladies had been put in comparative safety below the water-line, and the captain would have insisted that Count Lauritz remained along with them had he not reminded him that he bore the King's commission, and it was his duty to fight along with him and his men. So, kissing Eva fondly and begging the aunt, who was nearly dead from fright, to be of good cheer as they hoped to come out victors, he went on deck and then occupied himself with the sailors in strengthening their defences, for it was part of the captain's policy to let the pirates come on board and decimate them if possible at close quarters.

There were some thirty men or more besides the captain and Count Lauritz, good Danish sailors, each of them more than a match for half-a-dozen of the mongrel crew of desperadoes which formed the pirate's crew; possibly the pirate captain was aware of this, for he contented himself by firing into the "Dagmar" at intervals, hoping, no doubt, to cripple her in such a manner as to render her an easy prey when defenceless. Already two of her men had been slightly wounded by splinters, and much more damage might have been done if the captain, who, from the manner in which he handled his ship under such difficulties, seemed to be acquainted with their ways, had not lined that portion of his bulwarks, where his men lay snugly hidden, with some bales of clothing belonging to his cargo, and which effectually prevented the shot from passing through that part of his vessel. By-and-bye the pirate schooner came within hailing distance of him.

"What ship is that?" yelled the pirate captain through a speaking trumpet.

No answer from the "Dagmar."

"Lay her alongside!" yelled the pirate again.

No sooner said than done; grappling irons were thrown from the schooner to the ship, and, in less time than we have taken to write this, the pirate crew climbed up on the deck of the "Dagmar."

"Let them have it!" said the Danish captain. Bang, went one of the carronades, and a charge of grape tore a lane through the shrieking pirates, of whom those who were not dead or wounded rushed towards the quarter-deck.

"Again, 'Fire!'" shouted the Danish captain, and the second carronade vomited forth its deadly contents with such effect that scarcely a dozen were left of that crowd of howling vagabonds, so full of the lust of slaughter but a few moments before.

"Back to the schooner!" roared the pirate captain, seeing that he had been led into a snare, and that to remain another moment longer was to meet the same fate as his comrades, who were lying dead or wounded around him.

"Let them have it again," said the Danish captain, as all begrimed with powder he sighted the carronade himself, taking aim at the swivel-gun.

The pirates by this time had got on board their schooner, and, casting off the grapnels, began to crowd on sail to get away from the "Dagmar."

Bang, went the carronade again, and so true was the old sea-captain's aim that the shot knocked over the swivel that had done his vessel so much mischief ere the pirates had boarded them, and which might yet have proved their destruction, even though they had beaten them.

Probably the pirate captain understood this, as he shook his fist at him, and ordered the remnant of his crew to clap on all sail and be off.

By this time a stiff breeze had sprung up, and after all the dead pirates had been thrown overboard, the wounded looked after, and the vessel put to rights, the captain laid his course for Road Town, Tortola, where he hoped to find an English man-of-war to take him and his ship in safety to St. Thomas.

"His Majesty's High Commissioner is on board," said he, jokingly, to Eva, at dinner a few hours afterwards; "and it may be as well to take extra precautions to get him to St. Thomas to try the scoundrels who have so nearly taken my vessel."

He looked meaningly at Count Lauritz as he said so.

But neither they nor the mate told Eva that but a short while before they had received the dying confession of one of the pirates that Mr. James Teach was their head, and of all the miscreants who lived in St. Thomas by plundering vessels or exporting "Black Ivory," he was the vilest and most cruel.

CHAPTER V.

In the good old times of which we are writing, Road Town, Tortola, did a flourishing business. There were many fine estates upon the island, and quite a colony of well-to-do planters.

A great deal of sugar was made and exported, and its streets wore an air of business-like activity, that no one would believe to-day when they look upon its departed prosperity. It rejoiced in a Governor, and a numerous staff of officials, who lived in houses substantially built, and who spent their money in good living, like the gentlemen they were, until "Yellow Jack" carried them off, or they had saved up sufficient from their salaries to go home with a diseased liver, and end the few days that were left them.

It was in this friendly port that the "Dagmar" soon found herself, and when she had dropped anchor, her captain, accompanied by Count Lauritz, went on shore and paid his respects to the Governor.

This functionary, who had been one of His Britannic Majesty's naval captains before his appointment as Governor, welcomed them cordially, and his eyes twinkled with satisfaction when he heard from Count Lauritz how bravely the captain and crew had beaten off the pirates; but his countenance looked grave when he heard how deeply James Teach was implicated in the several acts of piracy which had been committed for so many years in those waters.

"I am sorry," he said, "I cannot lend you a sloop of war to accompany you over to St. Thomas, the two sloops of war which are generally lying here are out with the hope of catching a piratical schooner, which without doubt is the one you have beaten off. Perhaps if you remain a day or two and rest your men they may return. In the meanwhile, I am at your service during your stay in this island."

Returning thanks for his kindness they withdrew and went on board again, but they had hardly done so when two vessels hove in sight, one proving to be H.B.M.S. "Bulldog," and the other, one of Mr. James Teach's rakish-looking schooners, the one which had attacked them, with a prize crew on board, and a couple of pirates as prisoners; the rest had been slain along with their captain, who was cut down just as he was about to blow up his ship.

Perhaps by this time the reader may have divined why Mr. James Teach had leased Blackbeard's Tower, and the reason why he so punctually every morning spent an hour on the top of it, sweeping the horizon with his spy-glass.

He had grown frightfully anxious of late. All his schooners were away from the island, and as it was now about time for the "Dagmar" to be in St. Thomas, fears began to assail him that she might have been attacked by them, an eventuality almost too horrible to contemplate, for as his piratical associates invariably massacred all hands, irrespective of age, condition, or sex, it was quite as likely as not that the woman he loved was by this time at the bottom of the ocean.

For five long years her image had been before him. She occupied his thoughts to the exclusion of almost everything else. Curious anomaly; this man, who had never shed a tear within his remembrance, whose conscience was so deadened that he felt not the slightest remorse or compunction for all the murders of which he had been the instigator, was in this respect as tender-hearted as a baby, and he fairly trembled and wept at the thought of what might have happened to her. What is also very singular is the absolute surety that he felt of becoming her husband, and living a life of happiness hereafter. He actually believed it possible that such crimes as he had committed might be atoned for by a correct course of living in future. He never thought of being discovered, so long had he pursued his iniquitous career with impunity. He felt sure that his captains and crews were true to him, although he very much regretted that he had not disbanded them before sending for Eva.

It was when this agony of fear and apprehension was at its height, that one fine morning he beheld the "Dagmar," in company with a British cruiser, entering the port. Uttering an exclamation of joy as he caught sight of a beautiful young woman on deck, and whom he presumed to be Eva, he hastily descended the ladder which led to the top of the tower, donned his best attire, and proceeding to what is now known as the King's Wharf, entered his boat, which, pulled by four stout oarsmen, soon reached the ship.

"Arrest that man!" said the captain of the "Dagmar," as his foot touched the deck. Instantly he was seized, and before he could make the slightest resistance his arms were pinioned behind his back.

"What means this outrage?" he yelled, almost beside himself with rage and fury. "I came on board your vessel, sir, a peaceful Danish burgher, and you bind me as you would the meanest criminal."

"Just so," said the old Danish skipper, very quietly.

"Where's my ward?" cried Mr. Teach, foaming with passion and struggling to get loose.

But he was destined never to see her again. The one glimpse he had of her from the tower was all that he ever obtained of her in this life.

Count Lauritz had just completed his sad tale of her guardian's wicked career, as related by the dying pirate, when Mr. Teach was made prisoner.

Poor Eva, who though she had married without consulting him, and had calculated upon a pleasant meeting with him, was stunned at the news; and when the old aunt told her that all he had done for her was with the selfish motive of marrying her himself on her arrival, she wisely concluded, with her husband, that it would be best for her not to see him again.

All this time Mr. James Teach kept on insisting on an interview; from threats he used entreaties, until at last he almost humbly implored them to let him see her once more.

But the old captain was inflexible; it was only when he became more and more persistent that he turned to one of the sailors and told him to tell the lady's husband to step forward.

"Lady's husband!" exclaimed Mr. Teach. "You are joking. Eva married! Impossible! Let me go! What on earth have you bound me for? What——"

At this moment Count Lauritz advanced towards him. The sailors made way, those guarding Mr. Teach, slightly relaxing their hold. Then it was that an awful change came over his countenance. As he saw the Count he turned ghastly pale, almost livid; great beads of perspiration rolled down his cheeks.

"His ghost!" he said in terrified accents, recoiling as the Count came forward. "God in Heaven! Does the sea give up its dead? Away, I say!" and with a fearful cry, and a strength born of despair, he broke loose from his captors, rushed to the side of the vessel, and, bound as he was, threw himself overboard. His boat's crew tried to save him, but as a few moments afterwards the sea became reddened with blood, they concluded that a shark had saved the law the trouble of hanging James Teach.

Here endeth our story. We might have told a great deal more, if it were not for fear of tiring the patience of our readers. But with Eva married happily, and her aunt comfortably provided for, we think everyone ought to be satisfied. Nevertheless, some may like to know that they all lived to a good old age, highly respected in the Danish West Indies. The only thing worthy of note beside this is, that no clue could be obtained to the whereabouts of James Teach's immense fortune. It was always said that he had saved piles upon piles of Spanish doubloons. Their not being encountered after his death, led many to believe that he concealed them somewhere near Blackbeard's tower. Up to now, some people will not believe they were ever found. Some day, perhaps in a future story, we may tell how they were discovered.

"JAMES TEACH'S DOUBLOONS."

In looking over some old papers lately forwarded to me from St. Croix by my esteemed friend Algernon Divi-Divi, just before his departure for Europe with his aimable wife, née Miss Wigges, of Chicago, I came across the following history.

Written in a clerkly hand it bears the impress of that care which distinguishes most of the MSS. of the beginning of last century, and which, in this age of shorthand and typewriters, is becoming almost as rare as correct spelling was in those days.

Mr. Elias Divi-Divi, the grandfather of Algernon, appears to have been the writer, and he opens his story as follows:—

How I came to lay my hands upon James Teach's Spanish doubloons, is what I have never told anyone. Not even Rachel, the wife of my bosom, the companion of my life, the one human being who has always understood me and loved me, has ever known how I laid the foundation of my immense fortune, for at this moment of writing I am the owner of more than two thousand slaves and a third of the sugar estates of St. Croix.

I hardly know what prompts me to tell the secret—a secret which I have kept for so many years, even upon this paper— but a force impels me which I cannot resist. Perhaps it is the spirit of James Teach, who will not let me depart this life without letting the world know what became of his doubloons, the gold that he heaped up by his crimes.

As may be supposed by the reader of these lines, I was not always the wealthy man I am now. Most of those who came out to the West Indies when I did, were poor. As a rule they were white men. No coloured men came to us except those brought from Africa in slave ships, which traffic, though not permitted actually by the Danish Government, was more or less carried on as a profitable business by the merchants of St. Thomas, at which island I arrived when quite a young man. This was not very long after the death of James

Teach. The inhabitants had not yet forgotten the circumstances which attended it, and, often I have listened open-mouthed, and with a sense of terror stealing over me, to the awful stories they used to tell about him, and how disappointed the authorities were when they came to look for the huge fortune which his books showed that he must have accumulated during his residence in the Danish West Indies.

As a matter of course, the two old towers, Bluebeard's and Blackbeard's, came in for their share in these histories. They were in a sad state of dilapidation at that time, and such tales were told of lights having been seen flitting from one embrasure to another on stormy nights when no living being could have possibly climbed up to them, and of phantom processions, walking up the sides of the hill with huge sacks of money on the shoulder of each gibbering ghost, that young as I was, and fresh from the old country, and with the slightest experience of the world in which I lived, I would shiver again, and my teeth would chatter with affright as I thought of what might possibly happen to me at some time or other if I ever indulged in the morbid curiosity, which I had already begun to feel, to take a turn up to these relics of a century ago and look at them; perphaps obtain a clue to the treasure, which nearly everyone so confidently asserted was somewhere hidden near to them.

Not but what there were sceptics who laughed at those who believed in such idle stories, and who considered it a mere waste of time to indulge in such vagaries. Industrious and hard working men, most of them, they preferred busily to toil from morning till night in the great commercial houses which then controlled all the trade of the West Indies and Spanish Main, to digging for a treasure which might never be found, and of which, if even they discovered it, they would have to surrender the greater part to the authorities. I do not think it necessary that I should set down in these pages all that I passed through before I obtained sufficient means to establish myself as a money lender, not far from where the house of James Teach stands at this day; nor how I acquired my present knowledge of commercial affairs and the management of sugar estates. It is sufficient, I think, to state that I have been diligent, always so; no sooner have I got through one piece of work, than I immediately set myself about doing another, and if another were not at hand, to do something—read, write, or learn.

After I got over the fit of idleness which took possession of me when I first came to these countries, my common sense taught me that among a people whose sole aim was wealth, knowledge was power. I had no money, they had; my aim in life, therefore, was to learn how to get theirs in the easiest way possible.

And it was not so very difficult, then, for St. Thomas, besides being a busy hive of industrious merchants, was also the resort of countless visitors, natives of all countries.

Wealthy merchants from South America, returning to Europe to rest after long years of labour; officials from other islands, to retire upon their pensions, or to seek a change of climate for the benefit of their health; or, perhaps, a few young Cubans, with their pockets full of money, come up to St. Thomas to throw it away in the gambling hells, which held high carnival at that time, in one or two of its streets: or, perchance, a few pirates, slavers, or such like desperadoes, to spend their ill-gotten gains among the scores of lovely women that from more than one island came to join the birds of prey who lived upon such flotsam and jetsam as they were.

I cannot say that I made much head way with my fellow-townsmen; indeed, barring the one incident which I shall shortly relate, I do not really think I can remember anything of a very pleasant nature that occurred to me among them. Whether it was the profession I had chosen to adopt, I am not prepared to say. I always welcomed the needy, and I always lent money to them on good security, when I could get it; sometimes on bad, for a reasonable interest usually, more often an unreasonable one, according to circumstances.

I remember often taking myself to task frequently in those days for having chosen this way of making a livelihood, but I never could see myself in any other light than a public benefactor; putting it in this way: a man—whether through imprudence, misfortune, or otherwise; loses his substance—his first impulse like that of a man drowning, is to save himself. To do this he has recourse to his friends, ill-luck pursuing him, he tries them again, until they, dreading to be drawn into the same vortex of misfortune, refuse him. He then flies to the only door left open to him, that of the professional money-lender, who, if he exact good security and what the world terms an exorbitant rate of interest from the ill-starred individual, is scarcely to be blamed, when even those the most near to him have denied him.

I know there were some instances in which I did not figure so brightly before my sometimes awakened conscience, but there was no help for it, and I went on every day, not without a hope that the future would bring a change; for during the hours which this business spared to me, and I had little else to do but sit in my office and wait on customers, I kept on acquiring a knowledge of the many things which have proved so useful to me in latter days. It was about this time that dear Harry Thompson died. He was, as may be remembered, one of the most inveterate gamblers who ever played roulette or faro on the Main Street. A jollier nor more rollicking devil-may-care fellow never lived. To day rolling in wealth, to morrow cleaned out, after a night of it that would have killed a weaker constitution. On these occasions he would step into my office, and ask me for the loan of a hundred doubloons, which I am glad to say I was always ready to lend him.

Well, he was about the only mortal I cared for at that time, and one of the most honourable. I thought more of his word, than I did of all the papers and securities I had lying at the bottom of the old iron chest, I had so well filled in the corner of my office. In the same manner as the great houses of commerce lent thousands to each other whenever asked for, without a strip of paper or obligation, so did I lend Harry Thompson.

Only on one occasion did I loan him money on security, and that at his own particular request. It was for a very large amount, and whether it was that he had a presentiment of his approaching end or not, I cannot say, but he insisted on my taking the only house which was left to him as an indemnity should anything happen to him.

Of course I never expected anything would; he looked so hearty and cheerful when he took away the little keg of doubloons from my office; we did not use local banknotes in the West Indies; this piece of civilization had not yet reached us, but never in my life was I so horrified when I learnt the next morning that he had been stabbed to the heart by a vile

Portuguese, who, after cheating him out of every piece that he possessed, had adopted this dreadful means of ridding himself of his accuser when discovered.

As may be supposed there was a frightful uproar, out of which, the Portuguese escaped, only to be cut to pieces by the knives of Harry's friends, but as that did not bring him back to them, it seemed a poor consolation to have saved the hangman his labour.

At this piece of news I was inconsolable for some days. I liked Harry Thompson as I have liked but few men. So deep was my grief that I never thought of the large sum that I had lent him; and when the memory of our little transaction first flashed across me I had just finished my dinner, having done business for the day.

It was then I remembered the paper he had handed to me, and which, candidly, I had scarcely taken the trouble to look at.

I had put it away in my escritoire, not even in my strong box, of so little consequence had it appeared to me. But with my curiosity awakened to see its contents, I got up from my chair and walking into the next room where the escritoire leaned snugly against the wall, I pulled out one of the drawers, and possessing myself of the document, opened it.

As I did so a piece of paper fluttered out and fell on the floor.

Picking it up I read the following, written in the hand of my ill-fated friend:—

"DEAR OLD DIVI-DIVI,

"I feel as if something is about to occur to me that will put an end to our friendship for many a long day.

"Now you have always behaved very well to me. Yes, me, probably the most graceless dog ever born in these islands— and yet my dear D.D., I had a good mother who loved me, perhaps as yours did, and who when I was a little chap, without the knowledge of what a wicked world I had come into, taught me my prayers. Yes, as I have said before, for your kindness, in case anything should happen to me, I have transferred to you the title deeds of my house, the house which used to belong to James Teach, don't start—it really was his house, and if you have a mind to look for what there is to be found in it, you may possibly be able to solve the riddle of what he did with the doubloons. Of course, if nothing happens to me, the bargain is off—but none the less shall I be,

"Your faithful and obliged friend,

"HARRY THOMPSON."

"*P.S.*—As an aid to your search I recommend you to look at the piece of stuff which I have pinned to the letter.—H. T."

Attached to it by a pin was a small strip of parchment, on which were some singular characters.

It was not, however, till several weeks had elapsed that I installed myself in my new property.

It had not been inhabited for many years, and was sadly dilapidated. But after I had put in the plasterers, carpenters, and painters, and expended a few hundred pieces of eight[*], upon it, I found myself the possessor of one of the largest and best built houses in the town of St. Thomas. This was before the frightful fire which took place a few years afterwards, when nearly the whole of the houses and stores in the Main Street, were burnt down. Of course, such a place was much too large for me, but the idea of inhabiting so big a dwelling all alone was, on the whole, pleasing to me.

Perhaps I was influenced somewhat by the thought of the treasure which Harry Thompson had vaguely hinted was hidden within its walls. And I did notice that every now and again thoughts of it would intrude themselves upon me. This was at night, when I looked over the transactions I had made during the day. For with the acquisition of the house I had removed my office into the lower storey, where I found my business much improved, owing, no doubt, to its greater air of respectability. It was one evening in October, when I first made a careful examination of the strip of parchment to which I have already alluded. There was nothing very mystifying about it; a few zig-zags around the edge, a figure like a coffin in the right-hand corner, and some Arabic characters in the centre of an outline drawing of a house, very like the one in which I lived.

I had studied Arabic, and with little difficulty made out their meaning. This, however, was unimportant, and merely pointed

---

[*] A piece of eight was worth about 64 cents.

out that there existed a secret place in which James Teach's doubloons were securely stowed away. As I was already aware of this, I did not pay much attention to it, conceiving that, for some wise purpose best known to James Teach himself, he, for aught I know, might have got someone who knew Arabic to put those characters there merely as a blind to prevent anyone finding the money.

For a long time I pored over the strip of parchment, now and again approaching it to the lamp, which burnt brightly near to me, to see if its heat would not bring out other characters. But all in vain; not even the application of an acid affected it. So I gave it up in despair, throwing myself, somewhat fatigued, into my armchair, and trying to bring all my most serious attention to bear upon the paper before me.

It is possible that I may have remained reclining for some minutes, revolving every story I had read over and over again concerning the discovery of lost treasure.

At that moment there came a knock at the outer door. I looked at the clock. It was nearly midnight. Who could want me at that hour, I thought, as I took up the lamp from the table and prepared to answer the summons in person, my old housekeeper having gone to bed some time before.

But scarcely had I made a movement to do so, when the door leading to my office opened, and an African, nearly six feet high, and black as ebony, entered, closing it softly behind him. For a moment, I stood aghast. Whence had come this man, and at such an hour? And for what purpose? I am not naturally devoid of courage, but certainly the aspect of the fellow, who was armed with a heavy club, was so forbidding, that I felt my heart fail me—and, mind you, for the first and last time in my life before a negro.

There could be but one motive, I thought—Robbery! But how in Heaven's name had he got in? I had fastened up the house securely myself. Anyway, the cruel fact was there before me, in its most menacing aspect. It was well known that I had large sums in my possession, and no doubt the negro had been deputed by someone to rob and murder me.

Such were my impressions, as my visitor advanced a step or two nearer to me, all the time so gently and stealthily, you could not hear his footsteps. I fell back in my chair, overcome with such a fear as I had never felt before in my life.

Then it was he said, in the African tongue I knew so well, and upon the acquisition of which I somewhat prided myself—

"Be seated: I am not here to do you harm, but rather to explain to you the riddle which lies unsolved before you. Now, sir, if you can so far condescend as to listen to the words of your very humble servant—slave I have never been," here he drew himself up proudly, "no, not even when your cruel countrymen dragged me from my home in Africa—I will point out to you the use of that slip of parchment."

I rubbed my eyes: the tones of his voice sounded so far off and ghostly. Just then, the bell at the old clock tower tolled twelve, and had I been a shade more superstitious I might have thought that the flame of my lamp burned blue, and that the African was none other than Old Nick, in a duskier disguise than usual.

But he behaved very methodically for a ghost, and taking a seat opposite to me, with the table between us, he took hold of the slip of parchment. "There," said he, and he doubled the paper in a peculiar manner, "if you look at this, you will perceive the way in which James Teach built a portion of his house so that he might have a hiding place that no one might suspect. You see, he could not very well have used a cellar for the awful purpose for which he required it.

"This house is too close to the sea, and only a few feet down he would have found water. So he conceived the bright idea of building a place between two chambers, its flooring forming the roof of one, and its roof the flooring of the other. How to hide it was his masterpiece. This he accomplished by carrying along his staircase from one visible floor to another without taking into account the hidden portion of his dwelling. The entrance to it is not far from where you are seated. Maybe you would like to see it, but I warn you it is full of horrors; for when James Teach came to his untimely end, he left over a dozen of us, bound hand and foot and gagged, lying on the floor to die."

"To die!" I exclaimed. "But you are alive."

"Perhaps so," said my visitor, bitterly. "But it is only for the moment. I have a mission to fulfil. When that is done, I shall go back to the place that I come from."

I looked at him in amazement.

"I do not think you can conceive a more awful fate than ours," he continued. "We had already gone through weeks of torture and indescribable suffering in the ships which bore us to St. Thomas, but this was nothing to being left bound and helpless, without food or drink, in utter darkness, and not a soul to help us—for it was night when we were brought to this house. You can conceive our terror when we found no one came to our assistance, and what we must have felt as the hours dragged wearily along, we being bound hand and foot and gagged, and left miserably to perish. Oh! the selfishness of the villain who brought us here, taking his own life, without a thought of us poor wretches dying by inches up above."

I shuddered as I mentally reviewed the picture he had painted.

"Well, white man, some days must have passed, for by-and-bye the moans of my unfortunate comrades grew less. My wife and child were among them. The child had long since died, she told me, ere she, too, left us. Then I grew frantic and I struggled—aye, struggled until I broke the bonds which held my hands. At last I was free; but of what avail? I was in a room, ill-ventilated, surrounded by thick impervious walls, muffled so as to hide the loudest cry. I was almost as securely bound and gagged as before.

"Added to my misery, my companions who were yet alive besought me to end their sufferings. Mad with rage and despair, I seized the club which lay near by, and beat out their brains, ending my own miserable existence with a knife I found lying on the floor not far from where they died."

I was horror-struck. If this man or ghost's story were true, James Teach was one of the wickedest men that had ever existed. His gold could bring nought but misfortune. Again the negro, or his ghost, seemed to read what was passing in my mind.

"Nay, not so. The gold you seek has not sinned, though for its sake much sin has been committed. If it could harm you in itself, every piece that passes through your hands, and those of every man and woman living, would cause you harm: for every one of them is stained with more or less crime or virtue. As it is used, so will it cause good or evil. But I have said, I have a mission, and that is to take you to where we met our fearful end. There you will find our bones, as well as the iron chests in which James Teach placed his ill-earned doubloons. Gather up the relics of our poor mortality; bury them; and, if you can, say a prayer for us, as well as for the wilfully misguided wretch who made us suffer so. This done, you will be honestly entitled to all that you can find, and for this one good act to even the bones of a poor African you will deserve it, and no harm will come to you if you use this enormous sum of money charitably and well." Saying which, he rose, and walking to a round pillar which formed a support to an archway let into the wall, he touched a small projecting piece of iron, a portion of the pillar turned round, a staircase revealed itself, and motioning me to follow, I took up the lamp and did so. When I reached the top, my guide had vanished, and I stood alone, passing into a long, dark room.

There, just as the ghost of the African had told me, lay over a dozen human skeletons on their sides, not far from one another, crouching with their knees almost touching their chins. It was a gruesome spectacle, and for an instant my heart quaked within me, especially as close to me what must have been once the bony tenement of the African was lying stretched on the floor, the club not far from its fleshless fingers. And as he had said, there were the iron chests, four in number, chained strongly to the floor. My brain was in a whirl. There beyond a doubt were the doubloons of James Teach. I had but to open these chests to find them. But at that moment I was unequal to the task. I was alone, and, surrounded as I was by mouldering skeletons, and in a musty atmosphere, I felt sick and faint. The very air seemed alive with the spirits of the dead, muttering their sad plaints to me. How I got down from that chamber of horrors I can scarcely remember. I know I felt inexpressibly relieved to find myself next morning in bed, after a good sound sleep, alive, and in my senses.

Then the whole of what I have related came back to me, just like a fearful dream, which then I thought it was; but when on rising and examining the pillar and pressing on the small iron projection I found it turn, revealing the door of entrance and the flight of stairs leading to the room, I had to acknowledge to myself, if it were so, it was one of the most extraordinary that had been vouchsafed to mortal man.

It took me some days to remove the skeletons, which I did secretly, placing them in boxes and burying them at night. Needless to add, when I had successfully accomplished this, and prayed as I had never done before over them, I turned my attention to the four iron chests, which I found no difficulty in opening, as one of them contained a key which fitted each of them.

I shall not tell the amount of gold they contained, besides some lovely jewels, which I afterwards exchanged for the diamonds which my grand-daughter wears to-day. The gold was chiefly in doubloons and Spanish Joes, carefully rolled up in paper.

All these I carefully removed to my own strong-room below, and I can assure you they made a goodly appearance stacked upon its shelves, causing me many an anxious moment when I thought what the Government would do if they knew that I had got hold of James Teach's money.

But my secret was safe, and as I did not care to live any longer in St. Thomas, having met my darling Rachel when on a trip to Santa Cruz, I concluded to remove thither with my wealth, become a proprietor, and a useful member of the community. All this I did after my marriage, and with the help of my wife, who has been my constant companion through the cares attendant on such a stewardship, I think I may say with a clear conscience that I have given a good account of James Teach's doubloons.

"AN OLD COLONIAL GOVERNOR."

CHAPTER I.

ABOUT 200 years ago, when Jórgen Iwersen ruled the island of St. Thomas, Danish West Indies, with an iron hand, as befitted the first and one of the best Governors that it ever possessed, there resided among its scanty population of a few hundred souls, a man named Jan Weg.

He was one of the early colonists, and at the time our story opens, was owner of a large tobacco plantation and several houses on the one street, which at that time ran along the bay shore; he was also reputed to have saved a good many Spanish doubloons, acquired, so some of his envious neighbours asserted, by other ways than planting tobacco.

Before His Excellency, Jórgen Iwersen, arrived to take over his post as the superior authority in the island, Jan Weg occupied the first place in that little colony. This was partly due to his wealth, as compared to that of his fellow colonists, and his natural capacity to rule.

True, on more than one occasion, he had been referred to by the Home Government, when the islanders could scarcely be said to have had a head, so that may have had something to do with his assumption of the position. It had even been said that he looked forward to his appointment as Governor.

Be that as it may, it was a sore disappointment to him when he heard of Jórgen Iwersen's promotion to the office, and it was a bitter day in his household when it first came to his ears: for Jan Weg was one of those men who, for every slight inflicted upon them out of doors, always wreak a half an hour's misery upon their defenceless wives and children when they get home, even when they love them most dearly.

And Jan Weg was the lucky possessor of as good a wife and daughter as any man in that community. It must also be said in justice to him that they were first and foremost in his affection, and if he aspired to power and place it was that they should share it with him. Mrs. Weg had toiled early and late in helping him build up his present position, and their daughter, when she became old enough, had been a worthy helper. And women had to work in those days; talk of your *fin de siècle* women, as compared to our great great grandmothers, it is enough to make one's sides split with laughter to think of it.

They had to bake and brew, to wash and spin, to cook and sew, to keep accounts, to look after the slaves—both old and young, to make the pickles, darn and mend, to nurse their husbands and brothers when sick with the deadly fever, that only too often seized them on their first arrival at the colony, or when wounded by the Spanish buccaneers, to dress their wounds, and care for them. There were no doctors then, and thus it was that to them was given the task of learning the properties of the simples which grew around them, and of making and administering medicines to the sick.

And who is to estimate all that they passed through and silently suffered in the early days of these colonies, when so much had to be done to make their homes comfortable and life possible in the midst of that which was only too often hardship and privation? No one! Surely, not Jan Weg, who, a hard worker himself, let no one idle under his roof. Not even the dogs were suffered to pass their days in idleness. He actually trained a team to draw in and out of town the daily provisions for the plantation on which they lived; small blame to him for that, for are they not the greatest idlers in creation?

Thus it was that every soul under the roof which sheltered him and his family, worked from morning till night; each one adding by his labour to the goodly store which increased day by day around them.

It was a substantial dwelling that he lived in. Built on a hill; of solid masonry below and hard wood planks and mahogany rafters above; mahogany was plentiful in those days, and as it resisted the attack of the wood worm, it was frequently used for the purpose by those who could afford the time and labour to cut it.

A solid door studded with iron nails guarded the entrance. The lower story was occupied by a sitting room, and what would now be termed a pantry; smaller rooms were used as store and work rooms, and the upstairs as bed rooms.

The furniture was plain, home made but comfortable, more so, perhaps, than that of other colonists. An old fashioned clock, such as one may meet now and again in a Danish farmhouse, stood in one corner, a huge bible lay upon a shelf, a few old portraits hung upon the wall—his ancestors, so said Jan Weg—a half a dozen muskets were in one corner, and crossed in another were two broad-bladed swords, which rumour credited him with having used with deadly effect upon more than one buccaneer, when they made a foray upon the island in the days before he had gone hand in glove with them.

Tobacco and indigo were the produce of his plantation—tobacco principally, and of excellent quality. How it has died out in the island is a puzzle to those who read of the quantities they grew in those days.

Jan Weg himself was a sturdy Dane of fifty years of age. His wife had once been beautiful, but toil had somewhat marred her features, which, though seldom lightened by a smile, were comely still.

Their daughter Lisa was very fair to look upon. She was their only child, their darling. Stern and unbending to most men and women, Jan Weg was as plastic clay in the hands of his child. Did he frown, her lively sallies chased the frown away; were he wrathful, her pleading look soon made him peaceful; no matter what his mood were, she could change it as the harper does his melody, by a touch, the music of her voice, the magic of her smile.

And now Jórgen Iwersen had arrived from Copenhagen, and, as befitted the occasion, had been received with what ceremony the island could afford. Jan Weg had been the first to greet him; and those who saw them side by side could not help noticing how like in many ways they were to each other.

But while both men were grave and dignified as became their years and experience, to Jórgen Iwersen belonged that air of conscious superiority that comes only to those who are to the manner born.

Jan Weg seemed ill at ease. He had never basked in the sunshine of Court favour, and the many years he had led of toil and adventure in the colony made him feel instinctively that he was ill-fitted to cope with one, who with just as much experience gained in other climes, was a master of the arts of polity and government, such as they were then in Denmark. And this the little band of colonists soon found out a few days after his arrival.

Religious almost to fanaticism, arbitrary to a degree, edicts were soon promulgated, which while they excited much comment, were speedily obeyed. There was no shirking church under his rule, for every person who spoke Danish, and every one who did not, were bound to attend service every Sunday in Christiansfort when the drum beat, under a penalty of twenty-five pounds of tobacco. No longer was it permitted to a planter or a householder to keep his servants at work on Sunday. It had to be done on Saturday, under a fine of fifty pounds of tobacco. Every man had to hold himself in readiness to defend his owner or the colony at the first alarm given by a neighbour, or at the fort. Nor could any one leave the colony without His Excellency's permission. Women were especially prohibited under very heavy penalties. White servants were not allowed to sell or barter, and innumerable fines were levied upon those who purchased from them or harboured them if they ran away from their employer. The few negroes that had been already imported into the colony fared far worse, and were often cruelly punished for the slightest offence.

Withal, Jörgen Iwersen was just, just to a degree, if he ruled with an iron hand; if he sometimes exercised his authority almost to the verge of oppression, he took good care no one else should do so.

Armed with full powers from His Majesty the King, he used them well, and to those who conformed to the laws he issued he showed favour, and at times could so unbend as to be a right pleasant companion, full of information and knowledge of the great world he had lived in, and of which so few of the colonists had ever heard, much less seen. Christiansfort was now under a fair way to be completed. Here Governor Iwersen resided, here was kept the Lutheran Church, then as now the State Church, and it was here mainly that the events I am about to relate took place.

CHAPTER II.

From the very first period of their meeting there was no love lost between His Excellency Jórgen Iwersen and Jan Weg. Both felt instinctively that one of two such men as themselves was one too many in the island.

Jan Weg had been so accustomed to have his own way in all that he ever undertook, that when he found himself thwarted in more than one instance by the application with unbending severity of one of Governor Iwersen's edicts, he fumed and stormed at home in such a manner that not even the influence of his daughter could appease him.

Mrs. Weg would sit spinning in the corner of the large sitting-room listening to his angry tones. She never thought of saying anything. She was a prudent woman, and knew that such angry moments as these, like her kitchen fire, would soon go out if fuel were wanting. Still it was with no small concern that she watched the breach become wider and wider between Jan and the Governor. She loved her husband dearly, and felt instinctively that not all his wealth nor influence would avail him should he ever come in open conflict with the superior authority. No one in these days can conceive the power that such a man as Jórgen Iwersen wielded. It was a power of life and death. His Excellency was responsible to no one but his King, and, let us add, his conscience, which undoubtedly was his chief point of excellence. To do right was his motto, and he acted up to it with a force of character which is so admirable in any man, but when coupled with the stern integrity of the hardy Norseman almost verges on the sublime.

But Mrs. Weg, for all this, never interfered. She never broached the subject. She thoroughly respected her husband, and shared his feelings to the utmost. His ideas were her ideas when it came to the test. And she would have willingly died with him for them, wrong or not, so much was she identified with him as the companion of his life. She was none the less happy, though, when she found out the power which Lisa had over him, and still happier when she brought back the good humour to that honest, rugged face, peace to that really noble heart that had loved her so faithfully and well.

Unfortunately Jan Weg's ideas on the subject of property, whether in white or black men, land or animals, differed widely from those of Governor Iversen.

Jan Weg held that what was his, what he had worked for, what he had seen grow up after he had planted it, was indisputably under his control, and that he had a perfect right to do with it as he pleased. While he cheerfully observed the Lord's Day before the advent of the Governor, he had never been so straitlaced as to deprive himself of a good dinner for want of a cook to prepare it. Thus it was when he found himself without his hot steaming joint on a Sunday, because no one dare light a fire to heat it, his rage was almost ungovernable, and he repeatedly defied the law which compelled him to such obedience.

Governor Iversen never failed to fine him when he could prove that he had done so, and when on one occasion he went so far as to assist a friend of his away from the island without first obtaining permission, he summoned Jan Weg before him, and after roundly rating him, put such a heavy fine in tobacco upon him that he departed almost speechless with rage and mortification, and had it not been for the two stout halberdiers present with their weapons, it is more than likely he would have slain the Governor on the spot.

From that day a change came over him. From being open, frank and above board in his dealings, he became crafty and cunning, and used every means by which he could thwart the aims of his Excellency Jörgen Iversen. He knew from his inmost heart that the Governor was working for the good of the colony, that martinet as he was in some points, he was an honourable man, quite as honourable as himself, but his imperious disposition could not brook a superior, and as the island had not got along so badly under his own management, he fancied that these innovations were superfluous. He forgot how necessary it was for discipline and obedience among so few, exposed as they were to the inroads of the buccaneers, towards whom the sturdy Governor had shown an implacable front, hanging, drawing and quartering everyone that fell into his hands, whether bent on peace or war. And here was a great difference between himself and Jan Weg.

The latter when he ruled had temporized, and on more than one occasion when he should have chastised them for making off with some of his neighbours' stock, had let them go when caught with the payment of a small fine.

Rumour had it that he supplied them largely with cattle and food, and that at certain periods of the year his plantation was a rendezvous for them, and as from the hills close to his dwelling they could see passing ships with ease, they used it as a vantage ground whence to swoop down upon them when night set in.

Maybe this had reached the ears of Jórgen Iwersen, hence the coolness with which he regarded Jan Weg shortly after his arrival, and now that his Excellency had found occasion more than once to punish him for violating some of his recently issued edicts, the feud had grown so bitter that those who knew them best dreaded some day an outbreak such as never had been in the island of St. Thomas.

The Governor himself would have wished it otherwise, for he saw in Jan Weg a strong soul, who might have been of greater use to him in friendship than in hatred; but having once set his hand to the plough, his was not the one to draw it back again. So he redoubled his vigilance, established patrols along the country roads, watched carefully the incoming of strange vessels, their passing and repassing, and that so strictly, that it seemed next to impossible for any buccaneer to set foot upon the island.

For all his watchfulness they did contrive to elude him. Guided by Jan Weg through pathways only known to himself, from little bays around the coast that scarce any of his fellow colonists dreamt of, they held their meetings, bought his cattle and dealt with him just as if no such man as Governor Jórgen Iwersen had ever existed.

Now all this was innocent enough, until the captain of these lawless freebooters conceived the design of sacking the town and murdering all its inhabitants with the connivance of Jan Weg. He had already sounded him on the subject, when in one of his darkest moods against the Governor, and receiving no reply, had almost persuaded himself that he consented. Finding him as he thought a willing listener, one evening he fully unfolded his plot, expecting him then and there to enter into it.

Then it was the scales were lifted from the eyes of Jan Weg. He saw immediately the false position in which he stood towards these unscrupulous men, and what a frightful mistake he had committed by harbouring them. To hasten to Jórgen Iwersen and put him on his guard were his first thoughts, to alarm his fellow colonists the second.

Had the buccaneer only known the man he had to deal with, it is quite possible that he would never have unfolded his projects to him so openly, and had he dreamt for one moment of the intentions then flashing through his brains, with one swift stroke of his hanger he might have put him out of existence.

But Jan Weg was cautious. Recent events had made him so. Besides, these men had entirely misunderstood his quarrel with the Governor. If he passionately desired to revenge himself for the many slights he had suffered, he had not the least wish to bring destruction upon the colony. He was loyal to the backbone, and much as he hated the superior authority, would have been the first to lend a hand to repel a common invader.

So he courteously refused the robber captain, and bidding him good night, turned upon his heel towards his house. But he was not to escape so easily. The buccaneer had let him into a secret, a secret which once in the possession of any other would let loose the whole colony upon him before he could escape to his boats.

Where they stood just then was a wild and thickly-wooded portion of the country, not easy to traverse, and the way out of which he only knew imperfectly. What if Jan Weg were to betray them? To let him go thus were madness; so, making a sign to some of his men, who stood not far away from them, they precipitated themselves upon the colonists, and before he had a chance to defend himself had securely bound and gagged him.

CHAPTER III.

THERE was grief and dismay in Jan Weg's household at his non-appearance that evening. Mrs. Weg alone was aware of his having gone to meet the buccaneers, but never before had he remained out so late from home. In all things he was the most methodical of men, and insisting upon every one else under his roof tree keeping early hours, he always set the example.

The Fort gun* had long since fired, and it was already verging upon 10 o'clock before Mrs. Weg sent out messengers in search of him. She was well acquainted with the place of rendezvous, so there was no difficulty, if he were still there, of their encountering him.

Her anxiety, as well as that of Lisa, may easily be conceived, when they returned, declaring that he could not be found. One of them, however, had picked up a button, to which was attached a piece of cloth. This she recognised as having belonged to her husband's jacket. And when they told her that they had followed the footsteps of the buccaneers down to the sea-shore without finding any traces of him, her distress was redoubled. It was then that Lisa proposed to go to Jórgen Iwersen. In her heart of hearts she strongly suspected foul play, and that His Excellency was at the bottom of it.

Her mother thought differently. Her feelings toward the Governor were, that in such a crisis as this, he was the only one to help them. At the same time, she could not divert her mind of the idea that her husband had been spirited away by the buccaneers, either to hold until ransom were offered for him, as they had done before with other rich men of other islands, or that he had in some way or other become possessed of one of their secrets, and, fearing its betrayal, they had made away with him.

In either case, she was of opinion that nothing could be done before morning. Then they would institute another search, and, if they did not find him, they would seek the aid of the Governor.

She scouted anything like the idea of Jórgen Iwersen's behaving treacherously towards her husband. On more than one occasion she had met him, and with true feminine intuition she saw that he was far more inclined to be friendly than unkindly towards them. She bitterly regretted that she had not tried to bring about a reconciliation, for now she plainly saw that if her husband had really fallen into the hands of the buccaneers, he required such help as only that which a strong hand like Jórgen Iwersen's could extend to him.

So, dismissing her servants, she retired to rest with her daughter, but worried to a degree. They both loved him so

---

* To this day a gun is fired at 5 a.m. and 8 p.m., from the Fort.

that they imagined all things had befallen him. With all his faults, he had been a strong and helpful protector to both of them. Hard and exacting in some respects, but full of love and tenderness when the fit was over. Lisa wept freely as she pictured him, perhaps bound and shackled, in the midst of the savage buccaneers. She had heard awful stories about them. How cruelly they treated their captives, sometimes hanging them feet downwards over a slow fire, or applying thumbscrews to make them disclose where they had hidden their money: for in those days, as there were no banks, men and women buried their savings for fear of thieves, who, like the buccaneers, would not have scrupled to take them, could they have laid their hands upon them. And then when she had exhausted all that her imagination could conjure up of such pictures, she turned to console her mother.

She, poor thing, was sleeping a calm and sweet sleep, such as those without the slightest trouble or care enjoy. Lisa was astounded; had it been her husband, she never could have closed her eyes. She forgot how on one occasion in the early days of the colony her father's life had been in greater peril, and yet he came out scathless. Who knows if her mother did not anticipate the same good fortune for him once again, and with this hope had trustfully fallen asleep.

And so reassuring was the sight of her mother's calmness, that she, too, by-and-bye lay down beside her, and, like her, soon was in the land of dreams.

Mrs. Weg was up betimes, and, not caring to disturb her daughter, who still slept, accompanied by two of the overseers and a maid-servant, she proceeded to the spot where she knew her husband was accustomed to meet the buccaneers. It was a lovely morning. The wind blew steadily from the east, making the air delightfully fresh and cool. As yet the sun was only just peeping over the tops of the mountains, but the sky was sufficiently clear for them easily to see their way. A little rain had fallen during the night, just sufficiently to freshen up the landscape. But Mrs. Weg had no eye for the beautiful scenery which greeted them at every turn they took. Her thoughts were with her husband, and when, after a long and persistent search for him, extending down to the shores of the bay whence they were accustomed to embark, without finding any traces of him, she returned home more sorrowful than she had ever been since her marriage.

Her heart was heavy with its disappointment, and when she got back again and told how fruitless had been her errand, she burst into a flood of tears. In this she was joined by Lisa, and not a few of the household. When this outburst of grief was over, they decided to proceed at once to the Governor. Such an occurrence could not remain a secret very long, and it was policy, if nothing else, to be the first to acquaint His Excellency.

So, hastily swallowing their morning meal, they set out on foot for town, the roads being good and the distance not so very great.

Half an hour's walking brought them to it, or what the colonists were pleased to style such at that time.

A row of houses to the right of them, with patches of bananas and other fruits extending down to the sea shore, occupied the place where large warehouses are built to-day. At the end of the street was the Fort, then, as now, coloured red, and flying the Dannebrog from the tower.* Commanding the harbour and the town with heavy guns, visible from the ramparts, it looked formidable enough to Liza and her mother as they approached it. Scarcely any houses had been built upon the hills, perhaps from the fact that one Carl Baggert, who had begun to construct one, being ordered to remove it as it commanded the Fort.

Giving their names to the stout halberdier who guarded the entrance, and stating their desire to see the Governor, they were speedily ushered into his presence.

At that time the interior of one of the bastions had been fitted up for his use. The tower was not yet quite finished, or it was his intention to have occupied it in preference. He was an early riser, and nothing pleased him better than to get on top of it, unfinished as it was, to sweep the horizon with his spyglass, a new-fangled invention he had brought out with him from Denmark, and which had aroused no end of comment among his retainers, who were as much surprised as they were alarmed at its peculiar properties of bringing distant people close to them.

His Excellency had finished breakfast, and was in excellent humour. His nephew, a gallant seaman and captain of the

---

* This tower was pulled down some years ago.

one Danish armed vessel which then lay in the harbour, was standing near to him.

The Governor raised his eyebrows when the two ladies entered. He remembered Mrs. Weg and her daughter, who as a rare picture of loveliness no one really could forget, much less a connoisseur of beauty as His Excellency was known to be. Politely rising, he bowed. Curtseying to the ground, Mrs. Weg asked if she could have the privilege of a few moments' conversation with His Excellency. Motioning them to be seated, and bidding his nephew to remain with him, he graciously signified his assent.

Then Mrs. Weg told her story. How her husband had left her for an evening stroll, and how for once in his life he had not come home at his usual hour, and finally not at all. And then with fear and trembling, knowing that to conceal anything, even though it told against one so loved as her husband, would imperil any chances she might have of obtaining assistance from the Governor, she told him of her fears and suspicions, whilst stoutly maintaining her faith in her husband's honour and integrity. She felt sure, she said, that her husband had been carried away because of his opposition to their vile plots and plans, he had never gone with them willingly, she would swear to it.

Governor Iwersen's face during this recital was a study. At times he frowned, at others he had difficulty to restrain himself from betraying emotion at the sight of Mrs. Weg's genuine sorrow and her intense devotion to her husband. He scarcely looked at Lisa, who up to now had never spoken a word. The fact is, once or twice she found the gaze of the Governor's nephew fixed so ardently upon her that, colouring deeply, she held her eyes fixed to the ground for fear of meeting them. None the less did her heart beat quickly as she looked at him furtively from beneath her long eyelashes. She had never seen so handsome a man before, and, tricked out as he was in all the finery of a King's officer of that time, he was such a picture of a man as she had only seen in dreams.

At that moment, as if in confirmation of all that Mrs. Weg had said, the Governor's servant brought in a letter. Opening it, His Excellency read:—

"To Jórgen Iwersen. Greeting.

"Failing to get your head man, Jan Weg, to join us in sacking your Colony and hanging you at your own fort gate, we have determined to hang him, unless a ransom of 500,000 pieces of eight be not dispatched to us in exchange for him by to-morrow's sunset.

"JOHN MORGAN, Buccaneer."

The Governor had been so taken by surprise at this superscription that he had unconsciously read aloud the contents of this precious epistle, and he had scarcely done so when, with a heart-rending scream, Mrs. Weg had fainted.

Fortunately, Lisa bore it with more equanimity. It was nothing more than what she had expected, so she flew quickly to her mother's aid, and after a minutes application of restoratives had the happiness of seeing her come to herself again. In this she was aided by the nephew, much to the Governor's amusement, who, knowing him for one of the most diffident of men where women were concerned, had never seen him so assiduous before.

And would the reader believe it! This Old Colonial Governor was actually happy, rubbing his hands with joy, while those two poor women were shedding tears at the prospect of losing one so dear to them; yes, rubbing his hands for joy at the thought of the trouble Jan Weg was in, and how he, Jórgen Iwersen, the man he had so abused and hated, was going to be revenged on him.

"Ha! ha! Ludvig," he exclaimed, "get the ship ready at once, and be sure to take enough powder and shot to ransom our good friend Jan Weg from the hands of those rascally scoundrels who dare to hold such an honest man a prisoner. Happy! yes, I am happy as a king, to think I am going to bring you back your husband, and maybe," here he chuckled as he thought of his nephew, "a sweetheart for Miss Lisa. And now farewell, my sweet dames, to your home, and ere to-morrow's sun sets Jan Weg will know how well a Colonial Governor can love or hate.

CHAPTER IV.

THAT same afternoon Ludvig Iwersen set sail for the island, now known as Culebra. For some years it had been frequented by a band of buccaneers, who finding it the haunt of a number of wild-fowl and turtle had built huts upon one side of it and resided there, committing at times unheard of depredations upon passing ships and the neighbouring islands.

Hitherto no attempt had been made to dislodge them. Had Jórgen Iwersen felt himself strong enough, he would have attempted it long before. But, like a wise Governor, he had been busy strengthening his own defences and building his Fort, so as to be prepared at any moment against them.

But the arrival of his nephew in command of a fine ship of war, and the abduction of Jan Weg taking place almost simultaneously, offered him not only the means but the opportunity of wiping out this nest of depredators. Though scarcely warranted in doing so, owing to his position as Governor, he accompanied the expedition, feeling it was of too much importance to let his nephew, a new hand to the Colony, bear all the brunt of it. Besides, he was thoroughly conversant with the ways of the buccaneers, which were not always as fair and above-board as those of Denmark's sailors.

There was something so noble in the stand the Old Governor had taken towards Jan Weg, that it was with a feeling akin to admiration that Ludvig watched his uncle as he stood upon the high poop of his vessel. He had heard of the opposition, little short of rebellion, which his uncle had encountered at the hands of the chief colonist, and it was a matter of no small wonder to him that he had shown himself so willing to go to his aid. Then a vision of Lisa's lovely face came across him, and he asked himself if that had anything to do with it. And as he did so a pang of jealousy shot through him. But he had never heard of his uncle falling in love with anyone in Denmark for all the years of his long life; it would be passing strange if he had been caught by a girl born in the Colonies. Yet, stranger things had happened, and so his thoughts were beginning to run riot when his uncle called him.

"Ludvig" said the Governor, you are the captain of this vessel, and I am for the present your very humble servant," Ludvig bowed; "but it seems to me that with the gang of rascals that we are shortly to encounter it would be far better to try stratagem than force, so if you will allow me I will give you the result of my thoughts upon the expedition we have undertaken. There are two plans we might pursue; listen to them, and choose the one you like best. The first is to land a force from one side of the island, cross over, the distance is not great, and attack them in their huts. The other is to disguise our vessel as a merchant ship, pass boldly in front of them in the early morning and let them attack us; for as soon as they see us they will man their boats and do so, never expecting what a reception they will receive when once they board us. Now, I have carefully considered both of these plans. The first is not a bad one, but has its defects; they might, as soon as we attack them, kill their prisoner, whose life, after all, is what we principally wish to save. Then again, they will be fighting on their own ground, always a disadvantage to an attacking force, especially to men like yours, not used to tropical bush fighting. To my mind the second plan seems the best, for they will fall into a trap they least expect, and if we sink their boats by dropping a few heavy shot into them, and finish them off with grape as they board us, we shall kill or secure every one of them.

They will never think of killing their prisoner before they leave, not suspecting who we are.

To this Ludvig perfectly agreed, and as this method of fighting the buccaneers seemed most likely to be successful, steps were taken at once to make H.M.S. "King Christian," as much like a merchantman as possible. And so disguised, they sailed till evening closed around them, and the early dawn found them passing within easy distance of the buccaneers' rendezvous.

The buccaneers were on the look out, and no sooner did they see a strange sail passing, than they immediately prepared their boats for action. They took no account of the size of the vessel they were about to board; a braver and more desperate set of men never existed. A perfect lust for slaughter for ever possessed them, and it is recorded that when business was slack and there was no opportunity for appeasing it, they would fight duels, *à l'outrance*, among themselves for the booty they had won in their adventures.

Strangely enough, they had treated Jan Weg kindly during his forced stay with them; their usual custom, whenever prisoners fell into their hands, was to put them to unutterable tortures, in some cases for diversion, in others to make them tell where they had hidden their money. To stretch their limbs with cords, and beat them to death, to place lighted matches between their fingers, or to twist cords around their heads in such a manner that their eyes would burst out, were common practices. But in Jan Weg's case they had behaved towards him as if he were one of them. He shared their rude fare, their hard pallets, and living. In every respect he was well used as far as circumstances would permit.

Even the buccaneer captain had ventured upon a rude sort of apology for the rough treatment they had meeted out to him at first; even letting him into the secret of a treasure they had concealed on his estate, and promising him a share in it, if he would only join them.

To all this Jan Weg listened in silence, and knowing the character of the men with whom he had to deal, behaved towards them as if no breach in their former peaceful relations had occurred.

This conduct, with the prospect of a ransom for him, and possibly, the memory of many former acts of kindness may have had its influence; one thing is certain, when they departed in their boats to attack the seeming merchant vessel, many of them shook his hand in good fellowship, and the captain left him in charge of the camp.

Jan Weg watched them with straining eyes as they neared the object of their desires and boarded her like so many cats.

Then a singular thing happened. The strange vessel appeared suddenly alive with men, the buccaneers' boats disappeared beneath the waves, discharges of grapeshot, musketry, and small arms were repeated one after the other, then came terrific yells on the part of the buccaneers, who appeared to be fighting for their lives, then body after body was tumbled overboard; and finally, after what seemed to him a deadly combat, the smoke cleared away and all on board the good ship was quiet again.

Then, shortly afterwards, a boat descended from her sides, and was pulled towards the shore. In it were His Excellency Jórgen Iwersen and his nephew Ludvig, yet with the traces of hard fighting upon them.

When Jan Weg recognised the Governor, his heart fell within him. Not aware of his plans, nor of the pirates having sent him a letter, he could only suppose that he had determined to destroy this nest of pirates, and having done so, was coming to take possession of the plunder, and himself prisoner for joining them. His first impulse was to fly, but Jan Weg was a brave man. Then the memory of his dear wife and darling daughter came over him. Those thoughts almost unmanned him. At any rate, this tyrant of a Governor should see that to the last he defied him.

By this time Jórgen Iwersen had landed. To his intense satisfaction he had seen Jan Weg on the seashore, and had noted his first involuntary movement to leave the place where he stood.

"Who have we here?" he exclaimed, as he leaped out of his boat and advanced towards Jan Weg, who stood grimly regarding him, with arms folded across his chest, stern and implacable as ever.

"Jan Weg, at your Excellency's service," he replied.

"So! here Ludvig," said the Governor, an ominous frown appearing on his countenance. "Take this man prisoner. We have had enough of his contumacy, and by the saints he shall live to repent it."

"Live to repent it," thought Jan Weg, as he was quickly hurried on board the ship of war, "I expected death, but he said, 'I shall live to repent it.' Well, if he only knew the actual condition of my mind just now, I think he would know that my repentance was beginning already. I expected nothing less than a short, swift and speedy death. If he would only let me see my Katrine and kiss my Lisa once more, I think I could almost meet death with equanimity and feel better towards him, tyrant and despot as he has shown himself to be on more than one occasion."

But his reflections were soon cut short by the first officer informing him that the Governor had requested him to give his parole that he would not try to escape, in which case he would be left comparatively free until their arrival in port.

"My parole," answered Jan Weg somewhat bitterly, "whither could I go, should I try to escape? certainly not overboard to feed the sharks, who are yet, meseems, enjoying high carnival among the bodies of the buccaneers you have cast overboard."

The lieutenant smiled, and having obtained from Jan Weg the desired promise they became quite friendly, the officer inviting him on the quarter-deck or high poop, which did duty as such in those days.

From him Jan Weg learnt some of the details of the conflict — it had been sharp and decisive. The buccaneers had attacked them, quite unsuspecting the nature of the ship they were boarding; all hands had remained concealed until they showed themselves on the top of the bulwarks, when, in the twinkling of an eye, their boats were sunk by heavy shot dropped into them and their ranks decimated by a heavy fire of grape, the few escaping, being speedily despatched by small arms or tumbled overboard by sheer weight of numbers, as food for the sharks. The trap laid for them had been so successful that they had scarcely time to realize it, much less defend themselves, which they no doubt would have done had the surprise been less complete. The loss on the side of the King's men was comparatively small; indeed, they seemed rather disappointed that the skirmish had been so easily won, by which, it would appear that a Danish seaman in those days was as used to take hard knocks with equanimity as he is at present.

Not long afterwards the Governor and his nephew returned on board, Jan Weg was sitting somewhat disconsolately aft; he rose and saluted His Excellency as he came towards him.

"I am glad to hear, Jan Weg," said the Governor, "that you have promised not to escape from us, and, perhaps, as you may be hungry you will accompany us to breakfast, and, if so inclined, you may tell us how you came to join those rascals whom we have sent to their long account."

Jan Weg could scarcely believe his ears. The Governor had invited him to breakfast. Could this be the tyrant he had pictured in his mind for the past six months? And when, a few moments after, Ludvig informed him in the privacy of his own cabin that the Governor had actually planned this expedition at the request of his wife and daughter, on purpose to rescue him, his shame was too great for words, and big tears stood in his eyes as he faltered out his gratitude to His Excellency when they met at table, and how deeply he repented ever having given him cause for trouble or anxiety.

"Tut! tut! man," said this noble Old Colonial Governor, extending his hand to the now thoroughly conscience-stricken Jan Weg, "I only did my duty. You see there were other lives at stake besides your own. Your good wife—a peerless woman, your daughter—a charming girl, and, well I think I am not wrong in saying so, that of my nephew, who somehow or the other has not been heart whole since he has seen her, and whom, if the young lady be willing, I shall be proud to see her husband, with your consent, as soon as they can make up their minds to it."

Ludvig blushed a rosy red at the soft impeachment, being a seaman he was bashful.

Jan Weg swore that nothing in this world would please him better, and pledging His Excellency in a cup of the strong waters they manufactured in those days, vowed he would dower the young girl with the finest plantation in the colony, not to speak of a treasure which lay hidden on the shores of one of the bays attached to his own estate, and to which, now that the buccaneers were all dead, he considered justly his.

"You forget the State," said the Governor, "though as my nephew is entitled to something for the gallant part he has played to-day, I think the State may surely forego its claims; so we will endow them together. Your hand upon it, Jan Weg."

A few hours' sailing soon brought them to St. Thomas, where the news of their complete victory over the buccaneers was received with great joy, and Mrs. Weg and Lisa were awaiting their loved ones impatiently. Needless to say that it was a joyous meeting and that Ludvig and Lisa soon came to an understanding, for very shortly afterwards he asked her hand of her parents, and, if I am not mistaken, was married to her by Parson Slagelse in the Lutheran Church, then kept inside the Fort.

It was a joyous day in the colony. Everyone was glad to see Jan Weg and His Excellency on such good terms, especially Mrs. Weg, from whom a deep load of anxiety was removed.

That they were to live peacefully ever afterwards, would have been too much to wish for, as things went in those days. Let us hope they had a fair share of happiness. If they did not, it surely was not the fault of that iron-handed, good-hearted, Old Colonial Governor, His Excellency Jörgen Iwersen.

THE END.

A FEW WORDS ABOUT ST. CROIX.

(THE GARDEN OF THE WEST INDIES.)

GOLDEN GROVE, ST. CROIX, D.W.I.

A FEW WORDS ABOUT ST. CROIX.

(THE GARDEN OF THE WEST INDIES.)

PART I.

THE PAST.

ABOUT forty miles distant from the island of St. Thomas lies the island of St. Croix, another Danish possession, and one which has been known for many years as "The Garden of the West Indies."

It is easily reached from "Our Island of the Sea" either by one of the steamers of the Quebec Line, which touch fortnightly at St. Thomas, or by one of the schooners which ply twice a week between the two islands. A favourite is the "Vigilant," a trim craft with quite a history of its own, dating as far back as 100 years ago. She has been by turns a pirate, slaver, and a man-of-war; not a plank exists probably of the old "Vigilant" that was built in Baltimore about the year 1800, but the same beautiful lines and the same speed which made her famous as a slaver yet remain, and, to this day, she retains her reputation for these excellent qualities, though now engaged as a Government dispatch vessel and in carrying passengers.

Before leaving St. Thomas you are obliged to buy a passport. This costs 32 cents and permits you to pass freely to the island of St. Croix.

This beautiful island was discovered by Columbus on his second western voyage on the 14th of Nov. 1493. The Caribs, its inhabitants, called it Ay Ay; Columbus anchored there to obtain water, and while his boat was returning from the shore a skirmish took place with some of the natives, in which several of them were captured. These captives were carried to Spain. In 1625 the English and Dutch conjointly took possession of the island, which, at the time, was uninhabited. In 1649 the Dutch were compelled to leave the island, being driven from it by the superior force of the English. But the triumph of the conquerors was short. In 1650 twelve hundred Spaniards from Porto Rico made a descent upon them in the night, burned their habitations, massacred all whom they found under arms, and transported the remainder with their wives and baggage to the island of Bermuda. In 1651 the French, under De Vaugalan, obtained possession by the surrender of the Spaniards to his force. The island was then rich in forests, but these were set on fire by the new conquerors, and the conflagration, it is said, lasted several months. But the grounds thus cleared were at once entirely cultivated, and are said to have been "incredibly fertile."

In 1653 Louis XIV. transferred St. Croix with St. Kitts, St. Bartholomew, and St. Martins to the Knights of Malta. In 1665 a newly-formed West Indian Company purchased the island from the Order of Malta; and in 1674, this company having been dissolved by Royal Edict, the island was again annexed to the French Crown. In 1696 the population is said to have been 147 whites, exclusive of women and children, and 623 blacks, but, notwithstanding the extraordinary fertility of the land when the rains were sufficient, yet so frequent and destructive were the droughts at the time, that the French settlers, having demolished their forts, abandoned the island and removed to St. Domingo. In 1720 the island was uninhabited. About this time a project for its settlement was formed in England which was not carried into effect. It was visited by vessels of all nations till, in 1727, the French captured seven English merchant vessels which were lying there and took possession of the island. It continued to be the property of France till 1733, when it was sold to a company of merchants in Copenhagen, called the Guinea Company, for £30,750. The rights of this Company were afterwards purchased by the King of Denmark. In 1754 the island was carefully surveyed and divided into plantations. In 1801 it was taken by the British, but was restored to Denmark after

GOVERNMENT HOUSE, CHRISTIANSTED, ST. CROIX, D.W.I.

MARKET PLACE, FREDERIKSTED, ST. CROIX, D.W.I.

its possession for a few months only. Again in 1807 it was taken by the English, and was held by them until 1815, when it was again returned to Denmark.

During all these years slavery existed, though as early as 1792 the Danish Government declared the slave trade unlawful, and abolished it in 1803. But actual slavery remained in force until the year 1848, when the slaves, on July 2nd, rose in a body and obtained their freedom, which was proclaimed to them from the Fort at Frederiksted* by the Governor-General Von Shólten.

On Feb. 5th, 1866, a disastrous fire took place in Christiansted.† A great many fine buildings were destroyed and several families were rendered homeless. Then followed a long series of droughts covering a period of five years. The earthquake of Nov. 18th, 1867, was the next calamity which visited the island. It occurred about 10 minutes after 3 in the afternoon. There were two severe shocks, the sea receded, leaving its bed quite bare, and gathering itself in one mighty wave, came toppling over in immense rollers, carrying all before it. Schooners, brigs, and boats were washed ashore at both towns, and at Frederiksted a large American man-of-war, the "Monongahela," was landed high and dry on the Bay Street. Many lives were lost and much damage was done to property.

The next misfortune was a hurricane, which took place on the 13th of Sept. 1876; this destroyed a great many houses in town and country, besides injuring the crop. The next event of note was the so-called labour riot. For some years the negroes had worked under a law known as the Labour Act, a kind of contract between the negro and the estate owners, maintaining labour at a fixed price. Becoming tired of this an uprising took place on the 2nd of Oct. 1879, which resulted in a considerable loss of life and property. Estates were totally wrecked and nearly the whole of the town of Frederiksted was destroyed by fire.

---

* Also called West End. It is the port of call for steamers, about 15 miles from Christiansted, and is situated at the west of the island.

† The capital; sometimes called Bassin. Its situation is easterly.

There is not much left to chronicle after this event, except to note how rapidly the inhabitants of St. Croix set to work to repair their losses.

To look upon its smiling fields to-day, its prosperous towns and people, no one would believe that earthquake, fire, drought, and hurricane had ever visited it.

PART II.

THE PRESENT.

I DO not think that many people now-a-days know much about the inner life of the picturesque island of which I am writing. Tourists come and go, making a stay perhaps of twenty-four hours. A stray reporter or author writes a chapter or two about it, sometimes favourably, sometimes not, but rarely is sufficiently said to place its actual merits before those who seek health and pleasure in the West Indies. As the island of St. Thomas is justly famous for its magnificent harbour and unexceptionable coaling facilities, so is St. Croix for its climate, scenery, excellent roads, and the boundless hospitality of its people. It used to be visited annually by a number of Americans who came there for a change of air, its climate being well adapted to consumptives. How they came to exchange it for Bermuda can only be attributed to the proximity of the latter to America, which enabled them to reach it quickly. But now this is all changed, for one of the Quebec Line of steamers will bring you to St. Croix in five days, or should you be inclined only to touch at Frederiksted, the port of call, will carry you to every one of those "Islands of the Sea," that history has made memorable, or the pen of the traveller interesting. But should you remain, you will carry away with you recollections that will haunt your memory for years.

And you will not find yourself in a strange country. Though a Danish island, everyone speaks English; and you will be astonished, if you be an American, to find how the products of your own native land have invaded its houses and plantations.

A. J. BLACKWOOD'S STORES.
Agent for Bartram Bros.

A COUNTRY ROAD, ST. CROIX, D.W.I.

American furniture, toys, novels, magazines, dry goods, provisions, and machinery are largely imported. All over the country you will see the Cochrane windmill, or others similar, at work, and quite a number of America's best agricultural implements in use upon the estates. It would be an interesting task indeed to trace the cultivation of the sugar cane from the early days of the old cattle mill, and the very imperfect methods of making sugar among the ancient colonists, who, as Du Tertre, in his *Histoire des Antilles*, tells us, lived with their lives in their hands for fear of the buccaneers. I can, myself, remember many estates in the island dependent on the old windmill, with its cumbersome rollers standing on end and fed by hand by some poor negro at the risk of losing a limb. It was a red-letter day when the first steam mill was erected. It marked an area of improvement which has been kept up by planters ever since. Up to that time they had been content to follow the track laid down by their predecessors. But they were a sturdy race of men for all that, Irishmen most of them: honest and hard working to a degree; frugal in their habits, they worked unremittingly to amass a fortune, sometimes returning to their native land to enjoy it, but in most cases passing the rest of their lives honoured and respected in the land of their adoption.

It is said that money was easier to make in those days; prices were high, and even a small crop left a fair margin of profit, but from all I can gather, only those who were prudent and exercised self-denial were numbered among the successful. Dry weather would set in, or a hurricane, once in a while, would devastate their crops, bringing ruin and dismay to those who had not laid by for a rainy day. Few of these old pioneers are left. One of them, P. McDermott, Esquire, wealthy and respected, at the ripe age of eighty-eight, is yet living in the full possession of his faculties, hale and hearty, a fit representative of his hard-working countrymen, and a bright example of how long a man may live in the healthful climate of St. Croix. There are others that I wot of, as I pen these lines, Danish, Irish, and Scotch, whose lives would serve as a lesson to the rising generation. Those who know them, speak of them with respect and admiration for all that they did in the days gone by when steam and vacuum pans were unknown factors in sugar-making.

Life is a struggle under any circumstances, and even with the most approved appliances it is not always that the planter can make both ends meet. The beetroot sugar manufacture, bounty-fed and supported by the Governments of Europe, is a formidable rival to the sugar cane. Prices have gone so low, that in some instances it did not pay to make sugar, and the question has been so serious of late years as to threaten the entire industry all over the West Indies. It is gratifying to note that most of the planters have risen superior to the occasion, and, adopting the latest methods of cultivation and first-class machinery to take off their crops, are stemming the tide of adversity which of late years has set in against them. It cannot be too earnestly insisted upon that when a man is successfully opposed in business by another, he can only expect to maintain himself by adopting the methods of his opponent. Thus it is with sugar-making in the West Indies to-day. Those in Europe who have made the beetroot sugar a paying industry, have only done so by bringing every resource of science and art in its production. It is but natural to suppose if the West Indian planter would compete, he must go and do likewise.

This idea seems to be gradually taking root in St. Croix, where several of the large estate owners, by close personal supervision and attention to every detail, with improved machinery and methods, are turning out sugar at a minimum cost, and at a speed that would surprise the planter of a former generation.

One of the most notable examples is A. J. Blackwood, Esquire, who, as agent for Messrs. Bartram Bros., of New York, came to this island some twelve years ago and took over their business, which then consisted of two mercantile houses and several estates scattered over the country.

Up to that time, Captain Blackwood, as he is usually called by the community where he is known and so deservedly respected, had followed the sea as a profession, and from,

A. J. BLACKWOOD, Esq.

literally, before the mast, worked himself up to be a successful captain of one of the smartest vessels that ever plied between New York and St. Croix, enjoying to the full the confidence of his owners. He has said that it was with diffidence he undertook such a charge as was entrusted to him, but entering upon it with a strict determination to make it a success, and bringing to bear a natural aptitude for administration, which is all the more surprising from the fact that he had no previous commercial training nor any knowledge of sugar planting whatever, he has to-day the proud satisfaction not only of being a successful merchant, but of having erected one of the largest factories for the manufacture of sugar ever put up by private enterprise in St. Croix. This is at Lower Love, and is surrounded by eleven of the finest estates in the island. These supply it with cane, and, as seen from the fine residence of Captain Blackwood at Golden Grove, also planned and erected under his supervision, form a beautiful prospect. Far away is the ocean, of which you get a glimpse between the hills, many of which are cultivated to their summits. The fields are alive with busy workers cutting and carting cane to the mill. Little negro cabins peep out here and there from among the trees which grow near to them. Owner's or manager's dwellings and windmills, here and there, dot the landscape. Countless hues of green and brown greet the eye whichever way you may turn, from the sombre bistre to the dazzling emerald. Roads of a snowy whiteness intersect the island, completing a picture in which art combined with Nature has almost made perfect.

"So freshly fair are everywhere the features of the scene,
That earth appears a resting-place where angels might alight,
As if sorrow ne'er a visitant the human breast had been,
And the verdure of the summer months had suffered blight."

And now let us take a look at the works of Lower Love, whose great white chimney, standing out in the clear atmosphere, is seen for miles around.

Here, all is activity and life. Cart after cart comes in laden with the sweet-smelling canes. These are carefully weighed upon a great Fairbank's scale. Thence they are taken and placed upon the cane carrier, by which they are conducted to a first series of rollers which cut and crush them preparatory to their being crushed by the mill. Thousands of gallons of juice spout into the troughs, whence it finds its way into clarifiers, coolers, vacuum pans, and triple effects, going through a variety of processes before it becomes sugar, which, when made, is placed in canvas bags of 300 lbs. each, and marked to be shipped for refining.

The molasses is run off into tanks and barrelled, but not until a first, second, and third quality sugar is obtained from the cane juice. The "bagasse," or refuse from the cane, is burnt wet as it comes from the crushers and rollers. This is effected by a new process, and if it be considered that $10,000 every crop is saved by it in the manner of fuel, it speaks volumes for the new methods of manufacture so ably advocated by Captain Blackwood, and so thoroughly carried out at the works of Lower Love, a few words about the construction of which may be interesting. The plant of machinery was built by the Pioneer Iron Works, of Brooklyn, New York, and was erected on the Estate Lower Love, in the year 1893 by Chief Engineer L. H. Hansen, from plans drawn by Mr. Peter Penthony, who was then draughtsman in the Pioneer Iron Works. In order to erect this new plant it was necessary to re-construct the old building, which was done by Mason Wm. Peebles, under the supervision of Captain Blackwood. The main building, which was 100 feet long and 30 feet wide, is now 120 by 55. The old walls were raised 11 feet. In order to save the enormous expense for coal, by the introduction of green "bagasse" burning, it was found necessary to re-lay the boilers and build new furnaces or combustion chambers with hot-air flues; a large chimney of great draft-producing power had also to be built. This was effected by Mason Peebles, and, to-day, stands the finest example of such work in the island, its dimensions being 112 feet high by 7 feet diameter, inside measurement. This structure stands on a foundation of solid masonry 11 feet deep by 24 feet square. Its walls at the base are 6 feet thick and 18 inches at top.

SUGAR FACTORY

This plant of machinery is supplied with steam by a battery of five tubular rollers ranging in size from 16 by 5 feet in diameter with 54 four-inch tubes, to 18 by 7½ feet in diameter with 100 four-inch tubes, the furnaces being fed with green "bagasse" direct from the mill, which gives all the steam required with the consumption of about ¾ "bagasse" made, the balance being used up for manure. The grinding plant is composed of a set of three powerful rollers. These are 28 inches in diameter. This mill is fed by a Krajewski's cane crusher, which breaks, cuts, and crushes the cane, extracting about 40% of the juice, increasing the capacity of the mill from 50 to 100%, obtaining a juice extraction of about 70%. The crusher is driven by an engine 3 feet stroke by 16 inches in diameter, which also drives the cane carrier, the "bagasse" carrier being driven by the main engine. The evaporating plant is composed of an 8½ feet vacuum pan, with a 6 feet triple effect of the Relux type, driven by a pumping engine 3 feet stroke by 16 inches in diameter, and running ten pumps, which do the work of the entire plant. The cooling tower appears as an enormous fountain, and is run by a portion of the above-mentioned pumps. It draws the cold water from the bottom of the dam, passing it through the condensers which take the vapour from the vacuum pan and triple effect, returning the hot water to the top of the towers, where it falls from step to step, the air passing through it and cooling it in its descent, thus enabling the same water to be used over and over again for the same purpose.

The capacity of this plant is about 40,000 gallons of juice in 14 hours, which makes about 25 hogsheads of sugar of 1500 lbs., Danish weight, each. The molasses is separated from the sugar by a battery of four of Weston's centrifugals. This molasses is then boiled over and made into a second grade sugar, the molasses resulting from this is re-boiled and made into a third grade of sugar, which three grades of sugar give about 9 lbs. of sugar to 100 lbs. of cane. The washings of the house are then made into rum. It will thus be seen that nothing is lost, and every means employed to utilize the product of the cane.

Attached to this fine plant are machine shops, manager's and overseer's dwellings, negro cabins, &c., &c. There is a weighing house where every piece of cane is weighed before being carried to the mill, and every bag of sugar after it is made; every gallon of juice is measured, and the whole manufacture is conducted on scientific principles, being under chemical control; the laboratory being in the main building under the supervision of Captain Blackwood's brother, Mr. J. W. Blackwood, graduate from the Audubon Sugar School, Louisiana.

It is satisfactory to note how similar factories are beginning to be planned, one being about to be put up at Estate La Grange. This must be satisfactory indeed to Captain Blackwood, who, with their success, must feel his own assured. Let us wish it to him always, as we should do to every pioneer of progress, every investor of a great capital in manufactures, everyone who gives employment to the multitude, every man who overcomes obstacles and prejudices by sheer force of character, honesty of purpose, and a determination to do right on every occasion.

There are two towns in St. Croix, Christiansted and Frederiksted, also called Bassin and West End; that of Christiansted is somewhat old-fashioned, but has some fine buildings, the Government House being a massive pile that would do credit to a much larger city. The entrance to its harbour is very intricate, it is good and completely landlocked. As in "Our Island of the Sea," there is an old Fort, coloured red. A few guns peep over its ramparts, more for ornament than use, I suppose.

There is also a barracks for the soldiers, with a fine garden attached. There are several churches, a Lutheran, Episcopalian, Roman Catholic, and Moravian. There are no places of amusement, but with such splendid drives that the country affords over smooth level roads in the most comfortable of phaetons one passes the time most agreeably. There are comfortable boarding houses, that of Mrs. Pentheny being a favourite one for the officials and Americans. The house itself is finely built, three storeys high. The rooms are commodious, airy, and well furnished, and the table excellent.

STORES OF A. J. BLACKWOOD, AGENT FOR BARTRAM BROS.

Mrs. Pentheny is hospitality itself. Speaking of hospitality, this is a quality for which the West Indies and St. Croix in particular, are famous.

There are not many large commercial houses here. Captain Blackwood, as agent for Messrs. Bartram Bros. has a branch in this town. It is a large building, and a great deal of business is done there. There are several retail stores. An Ice Company has been lately established for the manufacture of that useful article. It owes its inception to Captain Pentheny and Mr. Canegata, the latter gentleman an enterprising merchant and proprietor. A great deal of aërated water is made and drank in the island, Mr. M. Pretto, another energetic storekeeper, turning out thousands of bottles weekly, besides owning and superintending a successful mercantile business. His residence is one of the finest on King Street, all the doors and bannisters being of solid mahogany. Messrs. Pretto and Canegata are natives of the Danish West Indies, and this reminds me that most of them are very intelligent, have a fair English education, and have filled and do fill many important places under Government. The Schools are very good, compulsory education being in force.

There is one newspaper, *The St. Croix Avis*, edited by John T. Quin, Esquire, F.R.G.S. An Englishman by birth, he has filled the important post of Inspector of Schools for many years. He is also Chairman of the Colonial Council.

There are an agency of the Bank of St. Thomas, a Club, and an Apothecary's Hall.

The Sheriff's Court, Dealing Court, and Police Court are conducted much on the same lines as those in St. Thomas.

The Central Factory stands just outside the town of Christiansted, not far from the Jail. It is carried on under Government inspection, and turns out a large quantity of sugar every year. We have alluded lengthily to it in a former work, "Leaflets from the Danish West Indies." It is satisfactory to note that it is now a successful if not a paying institution, being ably managed, employing a great many hands, and another illustration of how capital properly employed may benefit a community.

The "Farm" or hospital is romantically situated on the top of a hill overlooking the town. It is kept in a high state of efficiency by V. C. Haid, Esquire, the Superintendent, who gives a hearty welcome to anyone desirous of inspecting it.

Of the inhabitants themselves, a whole volume might be written. As I have said in "Our Island of the Sea," they are orderly and respectable. There is an air of comfort prevailing quite striking. The climate is equable, and no one is exposed to the vicissitudes of life which assail one in more populous centres. Labour is in constant demand, and those who are willing to work can always find something to do. More could be scarcely desired, except that wealth which does not often bring happiness.

Now for a drive through the country to Frederiksted. Snugly seated in a phaeton you bowl along at a rapid rate. Passing the splendid residence of Bulowsminde, now the residence of Robert Armstrong, Esquire, and once belonging to His Excellency, Governor-General Von Schólten, you leave estate after estate behind you, new views of infinite beauty opening up at every turn of the road. There are sugar canes on both sides of you, long avenues shaded by stately palms with here and there trees, such as the flamboyant, all aflame with scarlet flowers, or the silk cotton with enormous misshapen roots, and long horizontal branches on which grow a multitude of parasites and air plants; flowers of all kinds carpet the roadsides. Now and then you meet a labourer, who respectfully salutes you. Then a great sugar cart wending its way, slowly along, drawn by six oxen and laden with two or three hogsheads of sugar, or may be a light and strong wagon, heaped up with sugar in bags, drawn much more rapidly by two mules: types of the new and the old way of doing things. And as you near Frederiksted, just outside the town, you come across a lot of women busily washing in the Gut, named facetiously by a friend of mine, "The public wash tub," of Frederiksted. Then you drive into the town, and away from the glare of the sun you may find yourself seated in the splendid room of the Club located on the Bay

STORES OF ROBT. L. MERWIN & CO.

Street fronting the roadstead. This is another outcome of the restless energy of Captain Blackwood, and is built over his large stores, forming a handsome addition to the many other fine buildings which adorn Frederiksted and the Bay Street in particular.

There are several commercial houses represented in this town, besides the large interests of Messrs. Bartram Bros. Messrs. R. L. Merwin & Co. occupy a fine store on the Bay Street, in which they do a fair share of the island's business. Mr. R. L. Merwin, their senior, is an American; young, energetic, and enterprising, he enjoys the respect and confidence of the community. A branch of Messrs. McDougal & Co., of St. Thomas, who have another in Christiansted, and the house of Melchior & Sons, Copenhagen, whose courteous representatives, Messrs. Dessau & Ford, are well known throughout these islands, are also on this street. Messrs. Pearson & Co., of St. Thomas, have also considerable capital invested in enterprises both here and in Christiansted, and the retail stores are quite numerous and evidently prosperous. What will strike a close observer will be to see how many of them are superintended by females. They are, all of them, of native birth, and some of them remarkable for their industry and capacity. Though this may be said of all Dano-West Indian women, who are a credit to their sex as housewives and for their intelligence.

Counsellor Faber, K.D., owns the Apothecary's Hall. It is well supplied, and has realised for its owner a handsome competence, which it is to be hoped he may live many years yet to enjoy. As in Christiansted there are churches of various denominations, all of which are attended on Sundays and holy days. The Crucians are a religious people, and think much of their parsons, who do excellent work among them, being their friends and advisers on all occasions.

There are a hospital and other charitable institutions. The hospital has been superintended for many years by H. N. Mallgrav, Esquire, and is a model of good management. An old red Fort fronts the roadstead to the east of the town. It has a history, more than one notable occurrence having taken place within or around its walls. From its ramparts was read by Governor Von Schólten the proclamation which made the slaves free in 1848. It was stormed by the rioters in 1879 at the time of the riots. At its gates, John C. du Bois, an English clergyman and British vice-consul, breasted the angry mob and tried to stay them in their mad work. Just outside, a planter, Mr. Fontaine, met his death at the hands of the rioters. And inside, when authority once more asserted itself, many of these poor misguided beings were shot to death, tied to trees, which yet remain to remind those who live in these days of what is the eventual result of rebellion against law and order backed up by the bayonet and rifle.

No one looking at the fine street running along the side of the sea would believe that only a few years ago it was laid in ashes with the greater portion of the town. It seemed impossible to me at the time when I first witnessed it, in 1879, after the awful scenes of riot, arson, and pillage which took place on the night of the 2nd of Oct., that it ever would be built again, and yet here it is better than before, with handsome buildings and a prosperous people inhabiting them ; proving what great resources are in the island if only properly directed.

The port of Frederiksted is a very busy one during crop time. The Quebec Line is represented by Major Moore, who occupies a spacious dwelling on the Bay Street, where he has his offices underneath. The steamers of this Company call there twice a month; also those of Messrs. Pickford and Black, for whom Messrs. R. L. Merwin are the agents.

Schooners and other vessels ply between Frederiksted, St. Thomas, and the adjacent islands, and the town is very lively when a party of tourists arrive from the United States; then every tropical product is in demand. Bay rum, fruit, and curios, with the famous conch pearl, find a ready market, and the owners of phaetons, horses, and buggies do a flourishing business with the new comers. American flags fly, and, if one might judge from the conversation, everyone has become an American for the time being. And this brings

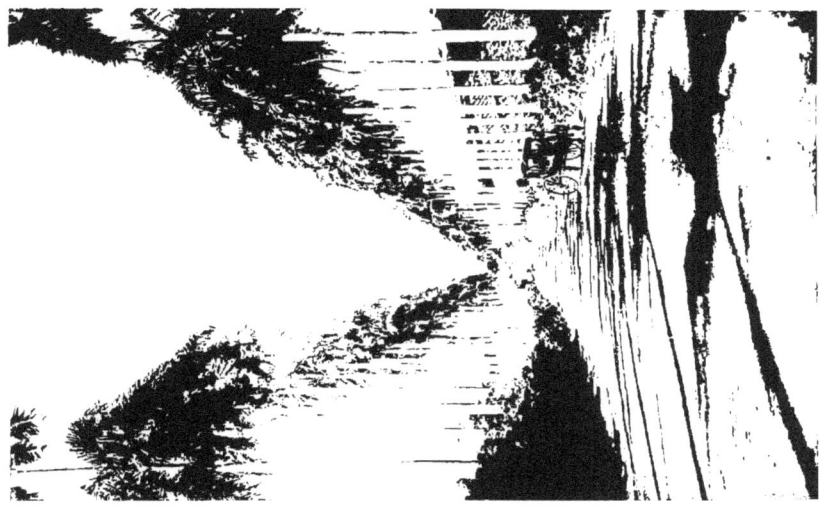

ROYAL PALM AVENUE.
St. Croix, D.W.I.

CHRISTIANSTED, ST. CROIX, D.W.I.

me to a subject which has been on the tapis for the past few years, a subject interesting to the writer and perhaps many more, and that is, the cession of these islands to the United States. I have already spoken about the possibility of St. Thomas becoming the naval and coaling station of America, and of the mutual advantages which might accrue therefrom.

Equally so would it be if St. Croix were included in the bargain. Its inhabitants are looking for it, especially those who have a considerable stake in the country. They feel that the mere fact of belonging to so great and commercial a nation means the infusion of new ideas, wealth, and prosperity. Not that they have aught to complain of the good government under which they have lived so happily, socially, and politically, for so many years. But there is a general impression all through the West Indies that the American flag will float over them some day; and it is believed that the Danish West Indies will lead the van. That America will not be a loser, as far as St. Croix is concerned, anyone who knows the industry of its people, its resources, the large amount of capital, American capital especially, invested in it, can testify. And then its enchanting scenery will more than ever make it a resort for the American, weary of old watering-places which outside of their fine hotels have grown flat, stale, and unprofitable. Here, amid the lovely green of its cultivated estates, its palm groves, or on its sea shore with its white rolling surf, will he find such delight, such variety and novelty as can be found no where in the world but in "The Garden of the West Indies."

www.ingramcontent.com/pod-product-compliance
Lightning Source LLC
Chambersburg PA
CBHW031448160426
43195CB00010BB/900